PEARSON

ALWAYS LEARNING

Doyle

Reading and Writing
Third Edition
www.els.edu

Taken from:

Ready to Read Now: A Skills-Based Reader
by Karen Blanchard and Christine Root

Eye on Editing 1: Developing Editing Skills for Writing
by Joyce S. Cain

Writing Academic English: Level 4, The Longman Academic Writing Series, Fourth Edition
by Alice Oshima and Ann Hogue

For Your Information 3: Reading and Vocabulary Skills, Second Edition
by Karen Blanchard and Christine Root

Reading Power 2: Extensive Reading, Vocabulary Building, Comprehension Skills, Reading Faster, Fourth Edition
by Linda Jeffries and Beatrice S. Mikulecky

Ready to Write 3: From Paragraph to Essay, Third Edition
by Karen Blanchard and Christine Root

Real Reading 2: Creating and Authentic Reading Experience
by David Wiese

Ready to Write 1: A First Composition Text, Third Edition
by Karen Blanchard and Christine Root

Get Ready to Read: A Skills-Based Reader
by Karen Blanchard and Christine Root

New Password 3: A Reading and Vocabulary Text, Second Edition
by Linda Butler

Ready to Read More: A Skills-Based Reader
by Karen Blanchard and Christine Root

Ready to Write 2: Perfecting Paragraphs, Fourth Edition
by Karen Blanchard and Christine Root

Engaging Writing 1: Essential Skills for Academic Writing
by Mary Fitzpatrick

What a World 2: Amazing Stories from Around the Globe
by Milada Broukal

More Reading Power 3: Reading for Pleasure, Comprehension Skills, Thinking Skills, Reading Faster, Second Edition
by Beatrice S. Mikulecky and Linda Jeffries

Writing to Communicate 2: Paragraphs and Essays, Third Edition
by Cynthia A. Boardman and Jia Frydenberg

Reading Power: Reading for Pleasure, Comprehension Skills, Thinking Skills, Reading Faster, Third Edition
by Beatrice S. Mikulecky and Linda Jeffries

World of Reading 1: A Thematic Approach to Reading Comprehension, Second Edition
by Joan Baker-Gonzalez and Eileen K. Blau

Vocabulary Power 2: Practicing Essential Words
by Kate Dingle and Jennifer Recio Lebedev

Writing to Communicate 1: Paragraphs
by Cynthia A. Boardman

First Steps in Academic Writing: Level 2, The Longman Academic Writing Series, Second Edition
by Ann Hogue

Writing to Communicate: Paragraphs and Essays, Second Edition
by Cynthia A. Boardman and Jia Frydenberg

Cover images courtesy of traffic_analyzer/iStockphoto and Kuklev/iStockphoto.

Development Project Manager: Courtney Towson
Production Project Manager: Theresa Festa

Photo Editor: Jamie Wilson
Associate Acquisitions Editor: Pamela Vitu

Taken from:

Ready to Read Now: A Skills-Based Reader
by Karen Blanchard and Christine Root
Copyright © 2005 by Pearson Education, Inc.
Published by Longman
White Plains, New York 10606

Eye on Editing 1: Developing Editing Skills for Writing
by Joyce S. Cain
Copyright © 2002 by Pearson Education, Inc.
Published by Longman

Writing Academic English: Level 4, The Longman Academic Writing Series, Fourth Edition
by Alice Oshima and Ann Hogue
Copyright © 2006 by Pearson Education, Inc.
Published by Pearson Longman

For Your Information 3: Reading and Vocabulary Skills, Second Edition
by Karen Blanchard and Christine Root
Copyright © 2007 by Pearson Education, Inc.
Published by Pearson Longman

Reading Power 2: Extensive Reading, Vocabulary Building, Comprehension Skills, Reading Faster, Fourth Edition
by Linda Jeffries and Beatrice S. Mikulecky
Copyright © 2009 by Pearson Education, Inc.
Published by Pearson Longman

Ready to Write 3: From Paragraph to Essay, Third Edition
by Karen Blanchard and Christine Root
Copyright © 2010 by Pearson Education, Inc.
Published by Pearson Longman

Real Reading 2: Creating and Authentic Reading Experience
by David Wiese
Copyright © 2011 by Pearson Education, Inc.
Published by Pearson Longman

Ready to Write 1: A First Composition Text, Third Edition
by Karen Blanchard and Christine Root
Copyright © 2010 by Pearson Education, Inc.
Published by Pearson Longman

Get Ready to Read: A Skills-Based Reader
by Karen Blanchard and Christine Root
Copyright © 2005 by Pearson Education, Inc.
Published by Longman

New Password 3: A Reading and Vocabulary Text, Second Edition
by Linda Butler
Copyright © 2009 by Pearson Education, Inc.
Published by Pearson Longman

Ready to Read More: A Skills-Based Reader
by Karen Blanchard and Christine Root
Copyright © 2006 by Pearson Education, Inc.
Published by Pearson Longman

Ready to Write 2: Perfecting Paragraphs, Fourth Edition
by Karen Blanchard and Christine Root
Copyright © 2010 by Pearson Education, Inc.
Published by Pearson Longman

Engaging Writing 1: Essential Skills for Academic Writing
by Mary Fitzpatrick
Copyright © 2011 by Pearson Education, Inc.
Published by Pearson Longman

What a World 2: Amazing Stories from Around the Globe
by Milada Broukal
Copyright © 2004 by Pearson Education, Inc.
Published by Longman

More Reading Power 3: Reading for Pleasure, Comprehension Skills, Thinking Skills, Reading Faster, Second Edition
by Beatrice S. Mikulecky and Linda Jeffries
Copyright © 1996, 2003 by Pearson Education, Inc.
Published by Pearson Longman

Writing to Communicate 2: Paragraphs and Essays, Third Edition
by Cynthia A. Boardman and Jia Frydenberg
Copyright © 2008 by Pearson Education, Inc.
Published by Pearson Longman

Reading Power: Reading for Pleasure, Comprehension Skills, Thinking Skills, Reading Faster, Third Edition
by Beatrice S. Mikulecky and Linda Jeffries
Copyright © 2005 by Pearson Education, Inc.
Published by Pearson Longman

World of Reading 1: A Thematic Approach to Reading Comprehension, Second Edition
by Joan Baker-Gonzalez and Eileen K. Blau
Copyright © 2009 by Pearson Education, Inc.
Published by Pearson Longman

Vocabulary Power 2: Practicing Essential Words
by Kate Dingle and Jennifer Recio Lebedev
Copyright © 2008 by Pearson Education, Inc.
Published by Pearson Longman

Writing to Communicate 1: Paragraphs
by Cynthia A. Boardman
Copyright © 2008 by Pearson Education, Inc.
Published by Longman

First Steps in Academic Writing: Level 2, The Longman Academic Writing Series, Second Edition
by Ann Hogue
Copyright © 2008 by Pearson Education, Inc.
Published by Longman

Writing to Communicate: Paragraphs and Essays, Second Edition
by Cynthia A. Boardman and Jia Frydenberg
Copyright © 2002 by Pearson Education, Inc.
Published by Longman

All trademarks, service marks, registered trademarks, and registered service marks are the property of their respective owners and are used herein for identification purposes only.

Pearson Learning Solutions, 501 Boylston Street, Suite 900, Boston, MA 02116
A Pearson Education Company
www.pearsoned.com

Printed in the United States of America

8 9 10 V031 17 16 15

000200010271295571

CT/JW

PEARSON

ISBN 10: 1-256-73981-2
ISBN 13: 978-1-256-73981-4

To the Teacher

Reading and Writing Doyle represents a bridge between the beginning and intermediate proficiency bands. In the beginning levels, students learn the fundamentals of writing a paragraph. As they advance through the intermediate levels, they will write essays in increasing levels of complexity. This book is divided into four units to correspond with the four weeks of the session.

The rhetorical style focused on in *Doyle* is Process, and the reading skills covered are previewing and predicting, identifying main ideas, and making inferences. Each unit has integrated reading and writing activities designed to promote reading comprehension, critical thinking, and discussion.

Unit 1 reviews the basics of paragraph writing, and introduces the rhetorical style of Process for a single paragraph. Unit 2 focuses on the reading skills listed above, with several writing activities which respond to the readings. Unit 3 guides the student through the process of expanding a single process paragraph into a three-paragraph process essay. The beginning of the unit provides an introduction to the American English style of essay writing, including the processes of prewriting, composing a first draft, and revising. Finally, the student is led through the steps involved in composing his or her own three-paragraph essay, and is presented with several model process essays. Unit 4 provides a capstone of both the writing and reading skills the student will have mastered by the end of the session.

Finally, the appendix offers some additional practice and reinforcement. It includes "Word Attack" skills with roots, prefixes, and suffixes, as well as spelling and punctuation rules, a chart of transition expressions, and an explanation of correction symbols. The appendix also provides some exercises designed to parallel the content of *Structure & Speaking Practice Dickinson*, including modals and gerunds and infinitives.

To the Student

Welcome to *Reading and Writing Doyle!* In this book, you will review how to write a paragraph and also learn how to write an essay in English. You will also learn some important new reading skills. The reading and writing skills you learn from this book will help you as you advance in your English studies. The book has four different units, and much more helpful material in the appendix.

Contents

Contents

Scope and Sequence

Unit	Reading Skills	Writing Skills	Rhetorical Skills	Vocabulary
1	Identifying parts of a paragraph; finding main ideas	Organizing a paragraph; writing a process paragraph; revising	Writing about a process; using the imperative	Time-order signal words; words about research and inventions
2	Previewing and predicting; reading for main ideas; making inferences	Writing in response to a text; writing predictions about a text; writing inferences	Anticipating the content of a text; articulating main ideas	Words related to humor and laughter; words about personality; words about shopping
3	Model process paragraphs; model process essays; making inferences; previewing; using a dictionary; identifying main ideas	Expanding a paragraph into an essay; writing a three-paragraph process essay; writing a thesis; writing an outline; brainstorming	Going from paragraph to essay; developing a thesis; word forms	Archaeological vocabulary; words about the workplace; words about relationships; synonyms; phrasal verbs
4	Making inferences; skimming and scanning; identifying facts and opinions; previewing and predicting	Writing about a process	Determining meaning from context	Words about superstition and beliefs; homonyms; synonyms and antonyms; words about trickery and deceit
Appendices	Reading about a process; determining main idea	Spelling and punctuation; editing	Modals, gerunds and infinitives	Roots, prefixes, and suffixes; transition words

Acknowledgments

The Third Edition of our ELS SSP and Reading & Writing texts is the culmination of nearly two-and-a-half years of hard work by countless individuals from ELS Language Centers in the US, Canada, and Australia. This project began in the winter of 2011 when we convened our Curriculum Revision Committee. The fourteen teachers, Academic Directors, and Center Directors who sat on this committee and saw the process through from start to finish are deserving of individual recognition for their tireless work: Lesley Carroll, Morgan Foster, Raylene Houck, Liz Hurysz, Dan Manolescu, Catherine Mason, Bernadette McGlynn, Mary McKay, Gerardo Mestizo, Scott Myers, Jim Scofield, Marie Silva, Carol Wright, and Lisagail Zeitlin.

This committee used their years of classroom teaching experience, study in curriculum design and ESL methodology, and intimate understanding of our ELS students to complete this tremendous task. The project involved, among other things, reviewing and refining specific language skills objectives for each level and text, reviewing hundreds of ESL texts, creating content, and organizing thematic units following a communicative approach to language instruction. Two sessions of piloting, five rounds of editing, and 27 months later, I am proud to present these texts to our ELS students.

I would also like to thank the 26 ELS centers and their academic teams that volunteered to pilot these texts, and over 50 ELS teachers who provided invaluable feedback. The feedback from teachers who used the texts gave us important insight into the practical use of these texts in the classroom and provided the basis for hundreds of edits and improvements.

A special thanks also to Terri Rapoport, Director of Curriculum Development, Susan Matson, Director of Teacher Training and Development, and Ward Morrow, Director of Academic Affairs, who, in addition to editing the texts, worked closely with our Curriculum Revision Committee and provided guidance, support, and advice.

In addition, we would like to thank Pearson Education, our publishing partner, for their collaborative effort in the preparation of the new edition. We'd also like to add a particular note of thanks to the Pearson Learning Solutions Rights Management group for their work in providing a significant amount of photo research for the series. The new photos help to shape the book and make it a more effective teaching and learning tool in print and digital formats.

Finally, thank you to all our academic staff and students for your belief in the power of teaching and learning English—and helping the world communicate better. May we all contribute to more peace, friendship, and understanding among all peoples of the world.

Mark W. Harris
President and CEO
ELS Educational Services

Unit One
Explaining a Process

WRITING 1

A. THE WRITING PROCESS

To get the best results when you write, break a writing assignment down into a series of steps and focus on one step at a time. The first step is **choosing a topic**. The second step is **brainstorming**, or gathering ideas. The third step is **organizing**, or putting your ideas in order. When you organize, you figure out what the main idea and supporting points are. The next step is writing the **first draft**. The final step is rewriting, or **revising**—which means rereading, checking, and improving your work to achieve a satisfactory **final draft**.

1. Choosing a topic

2. Brainstorming

3. Organizing

4. Writing the first draft

5. Revising

In the following pages, you will see how one student completed the chapter assignment by following steps, from choosing a topic to writing the first draft. As you read through the following steps, you will see how Miriam, a student from Israel, prepares to write a paragraph about one of her accomplishments.

B. Meet Miriam. Miriam is an international student in a Reading and Writing class. You will follow along as she goes through the process of writing a paragraph. First, Miriam makes a list of possible topics that she might write about. Second, she chooses the topic that she likes best. After that, she brainstorms, or writes down all of her ideas about her topic. Next, she organizes her ideas and writes the first draft of her paragraph. Finally, Miriam revises her paragraph, correcting all of her mistakes.

Above material from: *ELS Language Centers*

C. MIRIAM'S STEPS

Step 1 Choosing a Topic

Make a **list** *of things you have accomplished. Put a check (✓) next to the accomplishment that you think you can explain clearly in three to five steps.*

Miriam made the following list. She chose the last item to write about because it would be the easiest to explain in three to five steps.

I graduated from the cooking academy in Tel Aviv.

At my job at the hotel, I learned to cook meals for 200 people.

I learned how to use e-mail.

I got a visa to come to the United States.

I made a study plan for myself to get an associate's degree in dietetics technology.

On the first day of school, I learned the first names of all twenty of my classmates.

✓ *I set up a study place in my apartment.*

Step 2   Brainstorming

For the accomplishment you have checked, list the steps that you followed to reach it. You should have three to five steps.

Steps:

I chose a quiet place.

I found a comfortable table and chair.

I cleaned the area and took away my CD player and other things.

I put my school supplies where I could reach them easily.

I pinned my weekly study schedule on the wall where I could see it from my chair.

Step 3   Organizing

Look over your list of steps, and make sure that they are in the correct order and that you have not left anything out. At the top of the list, write a sentence that tells what you accomplished. This will be your topic sentence.

Miriam checked her list, and then she drafted a topic sentence:

To improve my study habits, I set up a study place in my apartment.

Step 4   Writing the First Draft

After reading Miriam's first and final drafts, begin your first draft. Start with your topic sentence, and complete the paragraph with supporting sentences that tell each step you took to reach your goal.

Miriam's First Draft

Draft #1	Miriam Pappan
	Creating a Place to Study
	To improve my study habits, I set up a special place in my apartment. I chose a place with good light and the right temperature. I cleaned the area and removed my CD player and other stuff, and I put my school things there. I put my study schedule on the wall so that I can look at it when I am sitting at the desk. Having a nice place to study has made me want to do my homework and succeed in school.

As Miriam studied the rest of this unit, she made some changes to her first draft. After finishing the unit, she typed her final draft.

Step 5   Revising

Miriam's Final Draft

> Miriam Pappan
> November 7, 2010
>
> ### Creating a Place to Study
>
> To improve my study habits, I set up a special place in my apartment. First, I chose a quiet place with good light and the right temperature. I can concentrate more easily in cool temperatures. Then I found a comfortable table and chair. Next, I cleaned the area of clutter and removed distractions like my CD player, photograph albums, and magazines. Then I arranged my textbooks, dictionary, paper, pens, and pencils where they are easy to reach. Finally, I pinned my weekly study schedule on the wall so that I can look at it when I am sitting at the desk. The study schedule shows the hours I attend class, the blocks of time when I study, and the times when I relax. It reminds me of my goals and responsibilities. Having a clean, functional place to study has made me more motivated to do my homework and succeed in school.

Above material from: *Engaging Writing 1*

READING 1

Process is a type of paragraph that explains how to do something. In a process paragraph, you usually write about the **steps** involved in doing something. Naturally, when you talk about steps, you list them in the order that you want the reader to do them. This always follows **time order**. Read this paragraph.

ANALYZING PROCESS PARAGRAPHS

A. Learning to Kick a Soccer Ball

Learning to kick a soccer ball well takes a lot of time. First, sit on the ground with your knees up. With your bare[1] foot, kick the ball up with the top of your foot. Be sure

---

[1]**bare** *adj.* without clothes or shoes

Unit One   Above material from: *Writing to Communicate 1*

that your ankle is locked[2] and that your toes are pointed. Do this until you can kick the ball up two feet and catch it on the top of your foot. Next, stand up, and do the same thing. Try to kick the ball up six or seven feet, catch it with your foot, and balance[3] the ball on your foot. After that, kick the ball against a wall. Practice this many, many times. Finally, put your shoes on and go through the same three steps. In short, if you spend lots of time and follow these steps, you will know how to kick a soccer ball well.

[2]**locked** *adj.* kept in one position
[3]**balance** *v.* to put something into a steady position without falling to one side or the other

What about you? Do you play soccer? What other sports do you like? Discuss this with a classmate.

Analyzing the Model Paragraph

1. What is the topic in the topic sentence?

2. What is the main idea?

3. How many steps are there?

4. Can you easily follow the steps? Are any steps missing?

5. How many major supporting sentences are there?

6. What words tell you that the sentences are major supporting sentences?

Above material from: *Writing to Communicate 1*

B. How to Send an Electronic Invitation

Read the paragraph and underline the topic sentence. Then answer the questions.

One of the easiest ways to send out invitations to a party is to use a website called Evite. First, go to www.evite.com and click on *create an invitation*. Then, choose an invitation from one of the hundreds they offer. After that, type in the details of your party such as the date, address, and start time. Next, enter all the e-mail addresses of the people you want to invite. Finally, check over the invitation and click *send*. You won't believe how easy it is and Evite automatically keeps a record of who is coming to your party. I recommend that you try Evite the next time you are giving a party.

1. What steps does the author give?

    a. _____

    b. _____

    c. _____

    d. _____

    e. _____

2. How are the steps organized? _____

SIGNAL WORDS

Many paragraphs include signal words to connect ideas in a paragraph. Signal words help guide the reader from one idea to the next.

When you want to explain how to do something, the first thing you need to do is make a list of the steps in the process. Then you should arrange the steps according to time order. When you write your paragraph, use time-order signal words to make the order of the steps clear to the reader.

1. *Review the examples of time-order signal words.*

TIME-ORDER SIGNAL WORDS			
first	first of all	next	second
then	finally	third	after that

2. *Complete the paragraphs using time-order signal words.*

a.   It's not hard to get a good picture of your cat if you follow these steps.

_____, give your cat something to eat. When she is full, move

your cat to a sunny window. _____, rub your cat's back for

a few minutes until she falls asleep. Do not make any loud noises. As soon as she

wakes up, get in position and have your camera ready. _____,

take the picture as she yawns and stretches.

b.   In order to get a driver's license in the United States you need to follow these

steps. _____, go to the Department of Motor Vehicles in the

state where you live and fill out an application. _____, study

for and take a written test on the traffic signs and driving laws. You also have to

take and pass a vision test. _____, you need to take a road

test. The person who gives you the test will make sure that you can drive safely.

Once you pass the road test, you will get your driver's license.

c.   It's easy to get driving directions from one place to another on the Inter-

net using a site called *Live Search Maps*. _____, open *Live

Search Maps* and click the icon that says "Directions." _____,

type into the "Start" box the address or location where you will begin your trip.

Unit One   Above material from: *Ready to Write 1, Third Edition*

_____, type into the "End" box the address of your desti-

nation. At this point, you can choose your route. To choose the quickest way,

click "Shortest Time." To choose the shortest way, click "Shortest Distance."

_____, click "Get Directions" and you will get step-by-step di-

rections from your starting point to your destination. Hopefully, you won't get lost.

Above material from: _Ready to Write 1, Third Edition_

d. _Complete the following paragraph using signal words._

It is very easy to make good popcorn. ____First____, put three or four tablespoons

of oil in a large heavy pot. _____, heat the oil on a high flame until one kernel

of popcorn pops when you drop it into the hot oil. When the oil is hot enough, pour

one-quarter cup of popcorn into the pot and cover it with a lid. _____, reduce

the flame to medium and begin to shake the pot gently. Continue shaking the pot until

all the corn has popped. _____, empty the popcorn into a large bowl and add

melted butter and salt.

Above material from: _Ready to Write 2, Fourth Edition_

IMPERATIVE SENTENCES

An imperative sentence expresses a command or a request. When we give someone
instructions, we often use imperative sentences.

You have learned that a sentence must have a subject and a verb. In an imperative sentence, the subject is always _you_, but it is not stated. Imperative sentences begin
with the base form of a verb and end with a period or an exclamation point. Look at the
examples. Notice that each one begins with a verb.

For negative imperative forms, we use: _Do_ + _not_ (OR _Don't_) + base form of the verb.

STATEMENTS	**Press** the start button. **Close** the door. **Add** the sugar. **Go** to the Department of Motor Vehicles in the state where you live and fill out an application. **Slow down!**
NEGATIVE STATEMENTS	**Do not** _make_ any loud noises. **Do not** _let_ the water boil. **Don't** _add_ too much salt.

Imperative sentences are often used in process essays.

1. Identifying the Imperative
Underline the imperative verbs in the paragraphs that follow.

a.　　Here are several steps you can follow to avoid jet lag. First of all, get a good night's sleep the night before you travel. Secondly, set your watch to the time of your destination when you get on the plane. Then, drink plenty of water during the flight. Don't drink alcohol or caffeine. Also, move around during the flight. Walk around the plane or do some simple stretching exercises in your seat. When you arrive at your destination, keep busy. Do not take a nap. Eat meals and go to bed when the local people do.

b.　　You can make perfect hard-boiled eggs if you follow these steps. First, take the eggs out of the refrigerator before cooking and let them come to room temperature. Then, put the eggs in a pan with enough water to cover them by at least an inch. Bring the water to a boil. Turn off the heat as soon as the water boils and cover the eggs for about 15 minutes. Next, put the eggs in a bowl with cold water and a few ice cubes. Let the eggs cool for 10 minutes. Now you are ready to peel the eggs and enjoy eating them.

Above material from: *Ready to Write 1, Third Edition*

2. Using the Imperative
a. *In the following paragraph, the pronoun* you *and several helping verbs are underlined. If they are not necessary, cross them out. Remember to use* don't *if the imperative is negative.*

BECOMING AN ATHLETE

　　If <u>you</u> want to be an athlete, <s><u>you must</u></s> take good care of yourself. First, <u>you must</u> get enough exercise. After <u>you</u> exercise your heart and lungs by running, <u>you must</u> exercise your muscles by lifting weights. Second, <u>you should</u> eat right. <u>You must</u> eat a lot of fruits and vegetables and other foods high in protein and low in fat. You need calcium, so <u>you should</u> drink milk, too. Third, <u>you must</u> get enough sleep every night. For most people, this means sleeping at least seven or eight hours every night. Finally, if <u>you</u> drink alcohol and take drugs, your body will become weak. Therefore, <u>you should not</u> take them. In short, after <u>you</u> follow these suggestions, you will be on your way to becoming a good athlete.

b. *What would you tell someone who is going to drive a car for the first time in your country? Write four imperative sentences.*

    1. <u>Follow the speed limit.</u>

    2. _____

    3. _____

    4. _____

What would you tell someone going on a job interview? Write four imperative sentences.

    1. _____

    2. _____

    3. _____

    4. _____

Above material from: *Ready to Write 2, Fourth Edition*

ARRANGING SENTENCES BY TIME ORDER

Discuss the pictures with a partner. Then, number the steps below the pictures in time order.

A. How to Remove an Ink Stain

1. 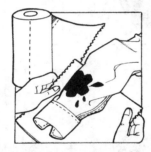 2.

3. 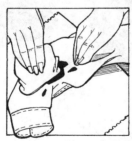 4.  5.

—— Then, spray the stain with hair spray.

—— After that, rub the stain gently with a clean cloth.

—— First, put a paper towel under the stain.

—— Finally, wash the piece of clothing as usual.

—— Continue rubbing until the stain is completely gone.

Read the topic sentence. Then, use the steps in Exercise A to complete the paragraph.

<u>This is what you need to do to remove an ink stain from clothing.</u>

_____

_____

_____

_____

_____

Discuss the pictures with a partner. They show how to carve a pumpkin. Read the list of steps after the pictures. Then, number the steps in time order.

B. How to Carve a Pumpkin

1.

2.

3.

4.

5.

6.

7.

_____ Next, draw a pattern for the face on the pumpkin with a felt-tip pen.

_____ Then, gently push out the cut-out features to the inside of the pumpkin.

_____ Finally, place a small candle inside the pumpkin.

_____ First, you need to make a lid. To do this, draw a circle about 6 inches in diameter on top of the pumpkin around the stem.

_____ Use a smaller knife to carefully carve out the face you drew on your pumpkin.

_____ Then, use a large, sharp knife to cut around the circle and remove the lid.

_____ After that, scoop out the seeds and pulp from inside the pumpkin with a large spoon.

Use the steps from the exercise above to complete the paragraph.

Carving a pumpkin for Halloween is fun, but it is also messy. So, make sure you have

covered your work area with newspaper before you begin.

_____

_____

_____

_____

_____

_____

_____

_____

_____

_____

_____

Above material from: *Ready to Write 1, Third Edition*

WRITING TOPIC SENTENCES FOR PROCESS PARAGRAPHS

The topic sentence of a process paragraph must identify the process and tell something about it. Write a topic sentence for the following paragraphs.

1. _____ First, get a copy of the receipt that shows you paid your tuition. Then take the receipt to the Student Affairs building. Go to the ID office and show the secretary your receipt. After that, get your picture taken. Remember to smile! Wait three minutes for your picture to be processed and your ID to be printed. Finally, sign your ID card and put it in your wallet.

2. _____ First of all, write your name and address in the upper left-hand corner of the envelope. Then write the name and address of the person you are mailing the letter to in the center of the envelope. This usually takes three lines. Put the name on the first line. Write the street address on the second line and the city and state on the third line. Remember to include the zip code. Finally, put a stamp in the upper right-hand corner. The most important thing to remember is to write neatly!

3. _____ First, fill a clean vase with water. Second, cut most of the flowers and greens so they are approximately two times the height of your vase. Then, cut a couple of the flowers two inches longer. After you are finished cutting the flowers, you can begin to put the greens in the vase. Now add the other flowers. Start at the outer edge of your vase. Put the longest flowers in the center of your arrangement. Then take a few steps back and admire your bouquet.

4. _____ First, put all the items you want to take on your bed and organize everything into groups. For example, put all your shoes in one group, all your clothes in another, all your underwear in a third, and so on. After that, place your shoes on the bottom of the suitcase. Then take your pants, fold them in half, roll them up, and place them in the bottom of the suitcase around the shoes. You can fill empty space on the bottom with socks and underwear. Next, fold and put flat items such as shirts and sweaters as a second layer. Finally, place your last layer of items in the suitcase. This way of packing helps you get organized and stay organized when you travel.

Above material from: *Ready to Write 2, Fourth Edition*

Paragraph form. Whenever you write a paragraph to hand in to your teacher, follow these guidelines.

- *Put the title on the top line in the middle of your paper. Always use a capital letter for the first word in the title. Use capital letters for all other words except for articles, prepositions, and conjunctions, such as* and *and* but.

  <u>A</u>n <u>I</u>mportant <u>A</u>ccomplishment for <u>M</u>e
- *Indent the first line of the paragraph five spaces.*
- *Use a capital letter for the first letter of the first word in each sentence.*
- *End each of your lines at about the same place on the right side of the page.*
- *If you are writing by hand, use lined paper with a margin line on the left. Except for the first line of your paragraph (which is indented), your writing should start next to the margin line.*
- *If you are typing, double-space and use a 12-point type size.*

Above material from: *Engaging Writing 1*

WRITING PRACTICE

1. *Choose one of the following processes to write about.*

How to:
- plan a party
- make your favorite dish

- change a flat tire
- get cash from an automatic teller machine
- study for an exam
- download an app on your cell phone
- plant a garden
- send or receive an e-mail

2. *Make a list of all the steps in the process.*

_____   _____

_____   _____

_____   _____

_____   _____

_____   _____

_____   _____

3. *Number the steps so they are in the correct time order.*

4. *Write a topic sentence that identifies the process and tells something about it.*

_____

5. Writing

Write the first draft of a paragraph describing the process. Begin with your topic sentence. Use the list of steps from your prewriting as a guide.

_____

_____

_____

_____

_____

_____

_____

_____

6. Revising

a. *Read over your paragraph and look for ways to improve it. Use the Revising Checklist to help you. As you revise your paragraph, think about these questions.*

1. Are your steps in correct time order?

2. Did you leave out any important steps in the process?

3. Did you use imperative sentences?

b. *Check for errors in grammar, spelling, and punctuation. Copy your revised paragraph on a separate piece of paper.*

REVISING CHECKLIST: CHECK YOUR WORK

1. My paragraph begins with a topic sentence.   Yes   No

2. My topic sentence identifies the topic and tells something   Yes   No
   about it.

3. I use transition signal words to show the order of the steps Yes   No
   in the process.

4. My paragraph has a concluding sentence.   Yes   No

5. I have checked my paragraph for . . .

   . . . ending punctuation after every sentence.   Yes   No

   . . . capital letters at the beginning of every sentence.   Yes   No

   . . . correct spelling.   Yes   No

Above material from: *ELS Language Centers*

WRITING 2
WRITING ABOUT HOW TO DO OR MAKE SOMETHING

A. PREWRITING

1. *Choose one of the following topics to write about.*
- how to pack for a weekend trip
- how to make a good salad
- how to fall asleep
- how to mend a broken heart
- how to cure the hiccups
- how to treat a cold
- how to convert from Celsius to Fahrenheit (or other metric to English measurements)

2. *Make a list of all the steps in the process. The steps don't have to be in order.*

_____ _____

_____ _____

_____ _____

_____ _____

_____ _____

_____ _____

3. *Number the steps according to time order.*

          Unit One   Above material from: *Ready to Write 1, Third Edition*

B. WRITING

1. *Write the steps from Exercise 2 on the previous page in sentence form. Use imperative sentences.*

1. _____

2. _____

3. _____

4. _____

5. _____

6. _____

2. *Complete this topic sentence about your process.*

It is _____ to _____ .
             (easy/fun/hard, etc.)

3. *Write a paragraph giving instructions. Use the list of steps from Exercise 1 above as a guide. Remember to begin with a topic sentence. Also, include time-order signal words to help guide your reader. Write a title for your paragraph.*

_____

_____

_____

_____

_____

_____

_____

_____

_____

_____

_____

_____

Above material from: *Ready to Write 1, Third Edition*

READING 2

As you read the article, complete the chart on page 17.

A. IT HAPPENED BY ACCIDENT

1   Many inventions happen when someone is looking for a faster, easier, or better way of doing something. They are the result of years of planning and hard work. But not all of them started out like that. Lots of inventions happened because of an **accident** someone had or a mistake someone made. For example, did you know that

ice cream cones, blue jeans, chocolate chip cookies, and Velcro are all the result of accidents? Some people have saved millions of lives because of an accident they had. Others have become rich by turning their accident into big business.

2   Have you ever eaten a Popsicle on a hot summer day? Popsicles were **invented** by accident by an eleven-year-old boy named Frank Epperson. In 1905, Frank accidentally left his fruit-flavored drink outside on the porch with a stir stick in it. During the night, it became very cold outside. Frank's drink froze with the wooden stick still in it. The next day Frank tasted the frozen drink. It was delicious. Eighteen years later, in 1923, Frank Epperson remembered his frozen drink. He decided to start a business making and selling the frozen drinks. He called them Epsicles, and he made them in seven fruit **flavors**. The name was later changed to the Popsicle.

"This is delicious. I wonder who invented Popsicles."

3   Many people use microwave ovens because they cook food much faster than regular ovens. But the first microwave oven wasn't invented because someone was trying to find a faster way to cook food. The idea of cooking food using microwave energy was discovered by accident. In 1946, an engineer named Dr. Percy LeBaron Spencer was **researching** microwaves. As he was working, he noticed that the chocolate candy in his pocket had **melted**. He guessed that the microwaves had caused the chocolate to melt. He decided to see what would happen if he put other kinds of food, such as popcorn and eggs, near the microwaves. He discovered that the popcorn popped and the eggs cooked. Spencer soon **realized** that microwaves cooked food very quickly. In fact, microwaves cooked foods even faster than heat. Dr. Spencer had discovered, by accident, a process that changed cooking forever. He went on to build the first microwave oven, which began a multimillion-dollar industry.

4   Penicillin has saved millions of lives since its discovery in 1928. But no one planned to discover penicillin. It happened by accident when a British doctor named Alexander Fleming was doing research on bacteria. One day Fleming was cleaning up his **laboratory**, and he noticed that a green **mold** was growing next to the bacteria. He looked at the mold under a **microscope**. He was surprised to find that the mold had killed some of the bacteria. Fleming

Mold growing in a petri dish.

thought the mold might be able to kill bacteria inside our bodies that cause many diseases. He was right, and soon the mold was developed into penicillin. Fleming said, "I did not invent penicillin. Nature did that. I only discovered it by accident." Today we realize that the discovery of penicillin was one of the most important events in the history of medicine.

5   So, if you ever feel bad because you made a mistake, just remember that some of the most important inventions in the world were discovered by accident.

IT HAPPENED BY ACCIDENT

Paragraph 2

Main Idea: _____

_____

_____

Paragraph 3

Main Idea: _____

_____

_____

Paragraph 4

Main Idea: _____

_____

_____

After you have read "It Happened by Accident," complete the exercises below.

B. CHECK YOUR COMPREHENSION

True or False? Write T (True) or F (False) next to each of the following statements. If a statement is false, rewrite it to make it true.

Example

___F___ Accidents never turn into big businesses. *Some accidents turn into big businesses.*

_____ 1. All inventions are the result of an accident.

_____ 2. Popsicles were invented by accident by a trained scientist.

_____ 3. Popsicles were first called Epsicles.

_____ 4. Dr. Spencer wanted to find a faster way to cook food.

_____ 5. Microwave ovens were revolutionary because they cooked food much faster than regular ovens.

_____ 6. Penicillin is an important medical discovery that was discovered by accident.

_____ 7. The antibiotic penicillin has saved millions of lives.

C. IDENTIFY MAIN IDEAS

Work in small groups. Read the following paragraphs and identify the main idea of each paragraph. Then choose the paragraph that could be included in the article "It Happened by Accident." Discuss the reasons for your choice. Did the other groups choose the same paragraph? Compare your answers.

1   Thomas Edison (1847–1931) was one of the greatest inventors of all time. During his life, Edison designed and produced hundreds of inventions. Sometimes he

Thomas Alwa Edison.

worked on forty inventions at the same time! Among other things, Edison is remembered for inventing the phonograph and the motion-picture camera. But in 1879, he showed the world his most famous invention—a light bulb powered by electricity. At that time, people used gas-powered lights to light their homes, factories, and streets. These lights were dangerous and inefficient. People were happy to replace them with the new, safer electric light bulbs.

Main Idea: _____

_____

2   Coca-Cola is one of the most popular drinks in the world. But it wasn't invented because someone was trying to find a tasty new drink. In fact, Coca-Cola didn't even start out as a soft drink. Dr. John S. Pemberton invented it in 1885 as a remedy, or medicine, for headaches. Coca-Cola tasted good, but it didn't work that well as a medicine. People eventually realized that Coca-Cola would be more successful as a soft drink than a headache remedy. So Pemberton added some other ingredients and sold it as a new soft drink. The rest is history!

Main Idea: _____

_____

3   In 1951, a woman named Bette Nesmith Graham was working as a typist, but she was not very good at typing. She made a lot mistakes and needed to find something that would hide her mistakes. This led to her invention of a special white paint. She brushed the white paint on her papers to hide mistakes she made. Her friends and other office workers heard about her white paint and bought it from her. Ms. Graham called her product "Mistake Out." She tried to sell it to IBM. Unfortunately for IBM, they decided not to buy it. Then, Ms. Graham changed the name to "Liquid Paper" and continued to sell it on her own for 17 years. In 1971, the Gillette Company bought Liquid Paper for $47.5 million.

Main Idea: _____

_____

     Unit One   Above material from: *Ready to Read Now*

D. TEST YOUR VOCABULARY

Choose the word that best completes each of the following sentences. Be sure to use the correct form of the word.

accident	laboratory	mold
flavor	melt	realize
invent	microscope	research

1. Don't eat that piece of bread! You should throw it away because it has _____ growing on it.

2. She is doing tests on rats in the _____.

3. I didn't spill the ink on purpose. It happened by _____.

4. The scientist is looking at blood cells under a _____.

5. Did Alexander Bell _____ the telephone?

6. He is _____ the effects of television on children.

7. Ice cream comes in many _____. My friend likes vanilla, but my favorite is chocolate.

8. The ice _____ when the sun came out. Now it will be safer for me to drive to work.

9. I'm sorry. I didn't _____ it was so late.

E. SUM IT UP

Summarizing is another important reading skill. Summarizing will help you remember the important information in what you read.

In your own words, summarize the accidental invention of one of the items in the article "It Happened by Accident."

_____

_____

_____

_____

F. EXPRESS YOUR IDEAS

1. *Discuss these questions in small groups.*

1. When have you made a mistake that turned out well for you? Describe the experience. For example, you may have learned something new because you did not follow the directions when you were cooking, driving, or making something in art class.

2. Which of the inventions in the article do you think was the best? Why?

3. Do you agree that all of these inventions were important? Why or why not?

4. If you could invent something to make your life easier, what would it be?

2. *Choose one of the questions above and write a paragraph about it.*

_____

_____

_____

_____

_____

Unit Two
Reading Skills

SKILL 1: PREVIEWING

A. WHAT IS PREVIEWING?

Previewing is when you look at something quickly before you read it. You preview when you want to get information.

Previewing means surveying a text quickly before you read it carefully. When you preview a text, look at the title and subtitles, pictures and graphics, words in bold print or italics, and introductions

Above material from: *Ready to Read Now*

Previewing is a common skill in daily life. You can preview many kinds of reading material.

For example, you might preview:

- the newspaper by reading the headlines
- a letter by looking at the envelope
- a new book by reading the front and back cover

B. WHY PREVIEW?

Previewing can help you make decisions. It can help you decide:

- which articles to read in the newspaper
- whether to open the letter (it might be junk mail you would throw out)
- if the book is interesting, and if you want to read it

In the same way, previewing can help you with your reading. When you preview a passage, you get some ideas about it. This way, your brain is already thinking about the topic when you start reading. You can understand better and read faster.

Previewing can help you with all of your reading. It is particularly helpful at school, for reading assignments and for tests.

C. How Do You Preview?

When you preview, you ask yourself questions about the passage.

The questions you ask depend on many things: what you are reading, why you are reading, and what you need to find out.

Some common previewing questions:

- What is it? (Is it an e-mail message, a news article, a piece of fiction?)
- Who wrote it and who is it for?
- What is it about?
- How long is it?
- It is difficult or easy to read?
- Is it interesting or useful?
- What will come next?

In these exercises, you will learn how to preview, and you will practice previewing in different ways.

1. *Read these first lines from a piece of writing. Then answer the questions.*

> Re: Your message
> Heard your message on my machine. Yes, let's get together.
> How about lunch . . .

a. What is it? _____

b. Who wrote it and who is it for? _____

c. What will come next? _____

Explanation

- We can tell from the way the writing starts (Re:) that it's probably an e-mail message.
- We can also guess that this person is writing to a friend because it's very informal. (An incomplete sentence, and expressions such as let's and how about . . .)
- This person will probably give a time and place for them to have lunch together.

2. *Read these first lines from different kinds of writing. Then answer the questions.*

1.
> **Ready to Go, Ready to Show!**
> 1993 Corvette Chevrolet
> Miles: 53,777   Condition: Like new   Asking Price: $14,400

a. What is it? _____

b. Who wrote it and who is it for? _____

c. What will come next? _____

2.

> Dear Sir/Madam,
> With reference to your advertisement on the JobFinders.com
> website, I am interested in . . .

   a. What is it? _____

   b. Who wrote it and who is it for? _____

   c. What will come next? _____

3.

> **The Dark Knight**
> Dark, complex, and unforgettable, this new Batman movie,
> directed by Christopher Nolan . . .

   a. What is it? _____

   b. Who wrote it and who is it for? _____

   c. What will come next? _____

Talk about your answers with another student. Are they the same?

D. PREVIEWING FROM TITLES

The title of a piece of writing is very important when you are previewing. You can use it to make questions about the passage.

1. *Work with another student. Read the title of a newspaper article. Then, write three questions about it.*

Peacekeepers Attacked

   a. _____

   b. _____

   c. _____

Explanation

Many questions are possible. Here are some possibilities:

- Who were the peacekeepers?
- Where were they attacked?
- Why were they attacked?
- Who attacked them?

2.

a. Work with another student. Read these titles of newspaper articles. Then, write three questions for each title.

1. _____ 88 Die in Crash _____

    a. _____

    b. _____

    c. _____

2. _____ Gulf Coast Hit Hard _____

    a. _____

    b. _____

    c. _____

3. _____ Channel Tunnel Slowdown _____

    a. _____

    b. _____

    c. _____

4. _____ Butterflies Losing Winter Home _____

    a. _____

    b. _____

    c. _____

> **Note:** The following exercises with a 🕐 have a time limit. You need to work quickly. Your teacher will time you.

*b. Preview the articles. (Read only the first lines and look <u>quickly</u> through the text.) Write the number of a title from **part a** above each article. You will have 45 seconds.*

1. _____

> Millions of monarch butterflies in central Mexico are in danger. Every year the butterflies travel from the Rocky Mountain area of the United States to the Mariposa Monarca Biosphere Reserve. This year illegal cutting has removed many trees from the reserve. If the butterflies can't return to the same area of forest as in the past, they may perish.

2. _____

> An Aeroflot passenger jet crashed yesterday as it was preparing to land at the airport in Perm, Russia. All 88 people on board were killed. The plane had flown in from Moscow to this city in the Ural Mountains. Russian officials said that the crash was probably caused by failure in one of the plane's two engines.

3. _____

> Train service through the Channel tunnel is likely to be slow for months because of work on the tunnel following last week's fire. The fire was the worst accident ever in the tunnel. It burned for 17 hours before fire fighters could put it out, and it caused serious damage to the north tunnel. The Eurostar trains and shuttle service will now run on reduced schedules.

4. _____

> Millions of people in Texas and Louisiana were left without water and electricity over the weekend after the passage of Hurricane Ike. The coastal areas were particularly hard hit. The city of Houston, which is the fourth largest in the United States, was almost completely shut down and empty. Around 2 million Texans obeyed orders to leave the coastal areas.

c. *Now read the articles and look for the answers to the questions you wrote in part a.*

d. *Talk with another student. Which questions were answered? Which ones weren't answered?*

PREVIEWING A PASSAGE

When you preview a passage, you read only small parts of it.

Which parts should you read? You should read the ones that will help you answer your questions about the passage.

Every passage is a little different, but you can usually find out a lot by:

- reading the title
- looking at any pictures or graphics
- quickly reading the first and last lines of each paragraph
- noticing names of people and places

PASSAGE ONE

1. *Read the title and look at the picture below. Write two previewing questions in the space provided.*

ARTIST MARIA ARROYO

1. _____

2. _____

 2. *Preview the article by reading only the underlined parts. You will have 30 seconds.*

   The <u>artist Maria Arroyo is having her first one-woman show in New York.</u>
<u>Born in Oaxaca, Mexico,</u> Maria attended art school first in <u>Mexico City</u> and then in
<u>Madrid, Spain,</u> where she studied with well-known artists such as <u>Orozco, Velasco,</u>
<u>and Murillo.</u>

5   <u>In the 1980s, she moved to New York and had several shows at smaller</u> downtown galleries. Then in <u>1985,</u> she went to live in <u>Brazil</u> with her <u>husband,</u> a journalist.
Her work in those years included many beautiful landscapes. They showed tropical
forests, animals, and mountains in very bright Brazilian colors.

   <u>Two years ago Maria moved back to New York.</u> <u>She</u> now teaches at the <u>New</u>
10 <u>York School of Art.</u> Last year some of her Brazilian paintings were included in a show
with other young artists. She has also shown her work in <u>Houston and Chicago.</u>

   <u>This new show includes some earlier work, as well as many new paintings.</u> She
has continued to paint landscapes, but now they are less realistic. The artist is more
interested in the colors and shapes than in real places. <u>The new work is remarkably</u>
15 <u>suggestive, and it proves that she is an important artist.</u>

3. *Work with your partner. Don't look back at the article. Can you answer your previewing
questions?*

4. *Now, go back and underline the words or phrases that helped you answer your questions.*

Unit Two   Above material from: *Reading Power 2, Fourth Edition*

PASSAGE TWO

1. *Work with a partner. Read the title and write two previewing questions on a separate piece of paper. Then show your questions to your teacher.*

ACCIDENT AT THE BROOKFIELD ZOO

 2. *Preview the article. You will have 45 seconds.*

Yesterday, a small boy was hurt in an accident at the Brookfield Zoo in Chicago. Thomas Kemper, 3, is at the City Hospital, but the doctors say he is doing well and will go home in a few days.

Thomas was at the zoo yesterday with his parents, Janet and Kevin Kemper,
5 and his baby sister, Sally, 6 months old. Janet Kemper says that Thomas loves going to the zoo, and he especially loves watching the gorillas. They went first to the gorilla area yesterday.

There are six adult gorillas and a three-month-old baby gorilla at the Brookfield Zoo. These animals aren't kept in cages. They're kept in large areas dug out of the
10 ground. These areas look very natural with rocks, bushes, and trees, but they have fences to keep the animals in and the people out.

According to Kevin Kemper, Thomas loves climbing and he'll climb anything. At the gorilla area, the Kempers were busy for a moment with their baby. In that moment, Thomas started climbing the fence.

15 Other people saw him and tried to stop him, but he was already at the top. Then when he looked down, he became fearful and he fell—into the gorilla area. He fell at least 18 feet, but fortunately, he didn't fall head first.

At this point, something remarkable happened. Before a zoo worker could arrive, one of the gorillas went over to Thomas. It was Binti Jua, the mother gorilla,
20 with her baby on her back. With one arm she picked up the little boy and carried him over to a door. Then she put him down so the zoo worker could get him.

Scientists at the zoo say they are not surprised about Binti Jua. A mother gorilla is not so different from a human mother in many ways. The director of the zoo has said that they will make some changes in the fences at the zoo, so accidents like
25 this cannot happen again.

3. *Work with your partner. Don't look back at the article. Can you answer your previewing questions?*

4. *Now go back and underline the words or phrases that helped you answer your questions.*

PASSAGE THREE

1. Read the title and write two previewing questions in the space below.

CHILDREN CAN'T STOP TALKING

1. _____

2. _____

2. *Preview the article. You will have 45 seconds.*

Two Spanish children are getting treatment for addiction[1] to mobile phones. The children, ages 12 and 13, went to a special center for problems of addiction. Their parents said they could not live without using their phones all the time. These are the first cases like this in the country.

5 The children were spending about six hours a day talking, sending text messages, or playing video games on their phones.

Dr. Maite Utgès, director of the center, said it was the first time they had treated children for addiction to mobile phones. She said that both children weren't getting along with other children and were failing at school. The children are now learning 10 to live without their phones. Utgès said they might need at least a year of treatment to get them off the mobile phone "drug."

Before they started treatment, both children had their own phones for 18 months. Their parents did not limit the time their children spent on the phones. The children paid for their phones by getting money from a grandmother and other 15 family members. They didn't explain what they were doing with the money.

Governments in other countries are also concerned about the way children use mobile phones. The Japanese government asked parents to limit the time children could use their phones. In Britain, doctors have reported several cases of children with problems because of mobile phones. In these cases, the young people became 20 very unhappy when they didn't receive enough phone calls.

A study in Spain found that 65 percent of children between ages 10 and 15 in Spain had a mobile phone in 2007.

[1]**addiction** when you are unable to stop taking something (i.e., alcohol or a drug) or to stop doing something

3. *Don't look back at the article. Can you answer your previewing questions?*

4. *Now go back and underline the words or phrases that helped you answer your questions.*

SKILL 2: PREDICTING

Previewing gives you an idea about what the reading is about and how it is organized. It also gives you an idea about the words that might be in the reading. The information you gain from previewing will help you make predictions about what to expect when you read. In this way, previewing and predicting are related activities.

Predicting is making an educated guess about what you are going to read. One of the goals of previewing is to help you make a prediction. You can also use what you already know about the topic to help you make predictions. Then, as you read, you can continue to make predictions about what will come next in the passage. Predicting is important because it keeps you actively involved in reading, and, therefore, helps you understand and remember more of what you read.

Above material from: *Ready to Read Now*

A. What Comes Next?

1. *Make predictions about what will come next. Circle the letter of the sentence that could come next.*

Example   Yesterday, there was a big snowstorm in Detroit. Many schools were closed, and people had to stay home from work.

    a. It was a warm, sunny day and the beaches were crowded.

    (b.) It was very cold, but the snow on the trees looked beautiful.

    c. Only one inch of snow fell in the downtown area.

The correct choice is *b*. Choice *a* is not correct. People don't go to beaches when there is snow! Choice *c* is not correct. In a big snowstorm, many inches of snow fall.

  1. There were many good shows on TV last night. The Smith family stayed home.

    a. They turned off the TV and went to bed early.

    b. The only interesting show was about traveling by bicycle.

    c. They saw a play, a music show, and the news.

  2. John and Alice Babson are not happy with the school in their town.

    a. Their children love to go to school.

    b. The classrooms are too crowded.

    c. It is a beautiful building.

  3. Many young people move to New York City after college.

    a. New York is a dangerous city.

    b. It's difficult to find jobs in New York.

    c. There are lots of interesting things to do in New York.

  4. Fly Happy Time Airlines! Take an exciting trip to Holiday Island!

    a. This trip is very expensive.

    b. Holiday Island has warm, sunny weather.

    c. Happy Time Airlines is never on time.

5. Alex had trouble falling asleep last night. He was awake until 3:00 a.m.

    a. This morning, he feels tired.

    b. This morning, he feels rested and ready to work.

    c. This morning, he is hungry.

6. The roads were covered with ice and were dangerous today.

    a. Sam drove home quickly.

    b. Sam took a long time to drive home.

    c. Sam enjoyed driving home.

2. *Talk to another student about your answers. Are they the same? Why are the other answers not correct?*

3. *Make predictions about what will come next. Circle the letter of the sentence that could come next.*

1. Tomiko got a cat last week. It's a pretty little cat, and it follows her everywhere.

    a. Tomiko can never find the cat.

    b. It even goes out for walks with her in the park.

    c. Tomiko's father doesn't like cats.

2. Sergio likes to listen to classical music in the evenings.

    a. Sometimes he falls asleep while he is listening.

    b. He works hard all morning and afternoon.

    c. His favorite kinds of music are pop and country.

3. Miriam and her brother, Peter, both go to dance classes.

    a. Peter likes to be different from his sister.

    b. Peter doesn't like dancing.

    c. Peter likes to do the same things as his sister.

4. My clock doesn't work very well. It's always a little slow.

    a. I'm often late for work.

    b. It's black with white numbers.

    c. It helps me get to work on time.

5. Rudy went to China last month. He didn't know how to speak Chinese.

    a. He didn't know any Japanese or Korean.

    b. Some Chinese people visited Rudy in Dallas, Texas.

    c. But a lot of Chinese people spoke English.

6. The weatherman on TV predicted cold weather on Saturday.

    a. I like to watch the weather report on TV.

    b. You don't have to bring any warm clothes this weekend.

    c. You should bring some warm clothes this weekend.

7. On Sundays, Gina's grandmother often cooks a big meal.

   a. Gina doesn't like cooking very much.

   b. She invites Gina and all her cousins for dinner.

   c. Gina doesn't see her grandmother very often.

8. Daren wants to go to Europe next summer.

   a. He says he is not interested in European history.

   b. In college, he is studying African history.

   c. He is saving money to pay for the plane ticket.

4. Talk to another student about your answers. Are they the same? Why are the other answers not correct?

Above material from: *Reading Power, Third Edition*

B. THE STORY OF TWO BROTHERS

1. Set a Purpose

The following story is an old Samoan folktale. Look at the map of Tutuila Island in Samoa. It shows where the story takes place. The two large mountains, Matafao and Pioa, are known as the Two Brothers. The folktale explains how they were created.

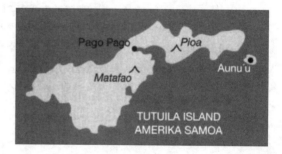

Write three questions that you hope the story answers.

2. As You Read

As you read the story, make predictions about what you think will happen next.

THE STORY OF THE TWO BROTHERS

1   Long ago, a man had two sons. He loved both children very much. One son he named Matafao; the other, Pioa. As small boys, they argued constantly. As they grew older, their fights became ever **fiercer** and more **frequent**.

2   Time passed. The father grew old. Tired of listening to his sons fight with each other, he began to lose hope. He knew the time was near when he would leave them. What would happen to his angry children?

Make a prediction. What do you think will happen next?

3   One day their father called Pioa and Matafao to him. This is what he told them. "My heart is heavy. It seems you cannot love each other as brothers should. In fact, every time you are together, one of you starts a fight. The only **solution** I can see is to separate you forever. Therefore, from today, you will live apart from each other. Pioa, you will live in the east," he said. "Matafao, you will live in the west. Perhaps the sea will be wide enough to keep you from fighting when I could not."

4   And then he added, "If either of you starts a fight, you will be turned into stone on the spot where you stand."

5   Soon the old man died.

6   Although the two brothers could not seem to love each other, they both loved their father. Their grief for him was great. In fact, they were so sad they could not eat. If their sadness had continued they surely would have died, too.

7   With the passage of time, grief lessens. So it was with them. The two brothers began to be happy again. They decided to have a feast. They would roast a whole pig and many chickens to feed the whole community. They would boil taro, a root vegetable, and bake a big cake.

8   Matafao and Pioa ate well at their feast. In fact, Matafao may have eaten a little too well. He decided to climb a cliff and look over his beautiful green **island**.

9   At that moment, high above their heads, a bird picked up a rock. The bird raised his great wings and flew up to the sky. When a strong wind blew, the rock slipped from his claws. The rock fell down the cliff and hit Pioa on the top of his head.

> Make a prediction. What do you think will happen next?
>
>
>
>
>
>

10   Pioa looked up. He became angry and **blamed** his brother, not the bird or the wind.

11   "It is your fault, Matafao!" Pioa screamed. "You threw the rock!" Then, he picked up a stone and threw it at his brother.

12   At those angry and unjust words, Matafao also got angry and threw some rocks. Rocks began to fly between the brothers, just as when a volcano erupts. Only then did they remember their father's **warning**, "Whoever starts another fight will be turned into stone."

13   Too late they found their father's words were true. Their legs had hardened and turned to stone.

14   Matafao realized then that fighting with his brother was wrong. He stopped fighting and **begged** his brother to stop, too. But Pioa was too angry, and he continued to fight.

15   "Stop, Brother. I beg you," Matafao pleaded again. When he saw that Pioa was ignoring him, Matafao fought back.

Make a prediction. What do you think will happen next?

16   It was at that moment that Pioa and Matafao became the mountains known as the Two Brothers. Pioa was humbled by his own wrongdoings. So, he became the smaller of the two mountains. The dark cloud that hovers over his head brings rain to the islands. "The Story of the Two Brothers" is still told to Samoan children. It teaches them several morals. For example, it reminds Samoan children to love one another. It also teaches that fighting is not a good way to resolve problems.

Reprinted from Faces Issue: Samoans. © 2002 Carus Publishing Company, published by Cobblestone Publishing. All Rights Reserved. Used by permission of the publisher.

3. *Look at the pictures that go with the story. They are not in the correct order. Number the pictures so they follow the order of the story.*

Now, write a short description of each picture.

C. FUNNY BUSINESS

1. The words in the box are boldfaced in the next article. Work with a partner and do the exercise that follows.

Words to Watch		
expert	humorous	burp
comedy	chuckle	embarrassed
examine	forbidden	insult

Idioms to Watch		
crack up	out-of-control	frowned upon
keep a straight face		

2. Match the words and phrases in the left column with the correct definitions in the right column. Write the letter of the correct definition. If you need help, read the sentence in the article where the word or phrase appears and think about how it is used.

Words

1. __d__ expert (n.)

2. ____ examine

3. ____ comedy

4. ____ insult (n.)

5. ____ chuckle (n.)

6. ____ humorous

7. ____ embarrassed

8. ____ forbidden

9. ____ burp (v.)

a. to look at something carefully

b. made to feel uncomfortable or ashamed, especially in front of other people

c. not allowed, especially because of an official rule

d. someone with special knowledge about a subject

e. a funny show

f. to make a noise through your mouth when gas comes up from your stomach

g. a quiet laugh

h. funny and enjoyable

i. a rude or offensive remark or action

Idioms

1. ____ keep a straight face

2. ____ crack up (v.)

3. ____ out-of-control

4. ____ frown upon

a. to laugh a lot at something

b. not possible to change, limit, or manage

c. disapprove of

d. to have a serious expression, even though you want to laugh

3. Preview

You are going to read an article about what makes people laugh. What do you want to learn about laughter? Write three questions that you hope the article answers.

Example

How do researchers figure out what makes people laugh?

1. _____

2. _____

3. _____

4. As You Read

As you read the article, make predictions about what you think will come next. Write your predictions in the boxes.

FUNNY BUSINESS

1   Laughter is part of every human culture.

> What will this section be about?

Like language, "it's a basic part of being human," says Robert Provine, a laughter **expert** at the University of Maryland in Baltimore. Unlike language, however, laughter does not have to be learned. Babies laugh when they are as young as three months old.

2   Provine and other scientists take the study of laughter and humor seriously. "After more than 27 years of study, I can now state with certainty what kinds of things will make us laugh," says Richard Taflinger, a **comedy** expert at Washington State University in Pullman.

3   Taflinger decided to **examine** a wide range of sources, from Shakespeare to *Mad* magazine. He studied thousands of hours of television comedies. Then he identified six basic elements that can make us **crack up**. Any **humorous** situation will involve one or more of these elements, he says. If something about one of the elements is not right, a joke will fail.

4   Humanlike behavior by nonhumans is one of those elements. Can you **keep a straight face** as you read about the other five? Look at the pictures for a **chuckle**.

5   The unexpected can be funny.

> What will this section be about?

A cow lying on the grass near a "No Parking" sign is a surprising—and amusing—image.

6   "A drawing of a dog chasing a cat won't get many giggles," says Taflinger, "but how about a mouse chasing a cat?" Now, that's unexpected.

7   **Out-of-contro**l situations can be funny.

What will this section be about?

In this scene from the 1950s television show *I Love Lucy*, actress Lucille Ball, on the right, and her friend are working in a candy factory. They are supposed to wrap the candy as it comes along a moving belt. But the belt is moving too fast. They can't work fast enough. As the belt speeds up, Lucy and her friend try to stuff candy into their mouths and uniforms. The more they struggle, the more we chuckle.

8   Doing something **forbidden** can be funny.

What will this section be about?

If someone **burps** out loud, especially in a quiet library, it would be **frowned upon**. You'd probably be **embarrassed**

if you did it. But your friends might laugh long and hard.

9   What's polite in one part of the world may be offensive, or impolite, in another, Taflinger points out. This is one reason people don't always laugh at the same behaviors.

10   Certain **insults** can be funny.

What will this section be about?

Sometimes insults are funny but, Taflinger explains, only if you are not emotionally attached to the group being insulted. How many little brothers does it take to screw in a light bulb? Look at the answer below. "This joke's funny only to BIG brothers or sisters," says Taflinger. "Little brothers would be insulted by it." ANSWER: Three (one to hold the bulb and two to turn the ladder).

11   Silly accidents can be funny.

What will this section be about?

When a fish bites the nose of film star Leslie Nielsen (who's only pretending to be hurt in this movie scene), people laugh.

12   "For something to be really funny, though, there must be no actual pain involved," says Taflinger. "It's humorous when someone slips on the ice and falls. People may laugh until they realize the person broke his leg. Then it's no longer funny."

SKILL 3: READING FOR THE MAIN IDEA

The **main idea** is the author's most important point about the topic. The main idea answers the question, "What is the main point that the author is making about the topic?" How do you find the main idea of a paragraph?

1. You need to read the paragraph carefully and identify the topic.

2. You need to ask yourself, "What does the author want me to know about the topic?"

Many times you will find the answer stated in one clear sentence. This is called the topic sentence.

The **topic sentence** states the main idea of the paragraph, and it is often the first sentence. This is usually the case in textbook paragraphs. But, the topic sentence is not always the first sentence. It can be the last sentence or even a sentence in the middle of the paragraph.

Above material from: *Ready to Read Now*

A. WHY ARE WE SHY?

1. *Read the first paragraph of the article "Why Are We Shy?". Then answer the questions.*

1. What is the topic of the reading?

   a. people

   b. shyness

   c. scientists

2. Based on paragraph 1, what is the main idea of the reading?

   a. Close to 50 percent of people are shy.

   b. Shyness is becoming more and more common.

   c. Scientists have some interesting ideas about why people are shy.

2. READING

First, look at the picture. Why might shyness increase because of the Internet? Then, read "Why Are We Shy?" below to find out.

WHY ARE WE SHY?

1   Are you **shy**? If you are, you are not alone. In fact, close to 50 percent of people are shy. Almost 80 percent of people feel shy at some point in their lives. These days, shyness is becoming more and more common. Now, scientists are trying to understand shyness. They have some interesting ideas about why people are shy.

5   Is it possible to be born shy? Many scientists say yes. They say 15 to 20 percent of babies behave shyly. These babies are a little quieter and more watchful than other babies. Interestingly, these shy babies usually have shy parents. As a result, scientists think that some shyness is **genetic**.

       Family size might cause people to be shy as well. Scientists at Harvard
10 University studied shy children. They found that 66 percent of them had older brothers and sisters. The scientists said that these children were often bullied[1] by their older brothers and sisters. As a result, they became shy. At the same time, children with no brothers and sisters may be shy as well. Growing up alone, they often play by themselves. They are not able to **acquire** the same social skills as children from
15 big families.

[1]**bullied**: hurt or frightened by someone bigger or stronger

Unit Two   Above material from: *Real Reading 2*

You may also be shy because of where you were born. When scientists studied shyness in different countries, they found **remarkable** differences. In Japan, most people said they were shy. But in Israel, only one in three people said so. What explains the difference? One scientist says the Japanese and Israelis have differ-
20 ent opinions of **failure**. In Japan, when people do not **succeed**, they feel bad about themselves. They **blame** themselves for their failure. In Israel, the opposite is true. Israelis often blame failure on outside reasons, such as family, teachers, friends, or bad luck. In Israel, freedom of opinion and risk taking[2] are strongly supported. This may be why Israelis worry less about failure and are less shy.

25   Technology could be another cause of shyness. As more and more people use the Internet, they spend less time outside, talking to people. As a result, they lose practice at conversation. Speaking to new people face to face can make them feel **anxious**. Scientists think this may be why the number of shy people in America has **increased** by 10 percent in recent years.

30   For shy people, it can be difficult to make friends, speak in class, and even get a good job. But, scientists say you can **get over** your shyness. They suggest trying new things and practicing conversation. And don't forget—if you are shy, you are not the only one.

3. VOCABULARY CHECK

Complete the sentences with the boldfaced words from the reading.

1. Something that has a bad final result is a(n) _____.

2. When you do something and you _____, you have a good final result.

3. If a problem stops you from doing something, you want to _____ it, or learn to control the problem.

4. When you _____ another person, you say that person is responsible for something bad.

5. If something is _____, it surprises you and you want to tell people about it.

6. Students often feel _____ before an important test.

7. If you have a good job and earn a lot of money, you can _____ a big house and a nice car.

8. If it is difficult for you to meet and speak to new people, you may be a(n) _____ person.

9. When something has _____, it has become larger in number or amount.

10. Something that is _____ is passed down to you from your parents.

[2]**risk taking**: doing something even though there is a chance that something bad will happen

4. READ AGAIN

Read "Why Are We Shy?" again and complete the comprehension exercises.

5. COMPREHENSION CHECK

1. *Read the statements about shyness. Check (✓) the statements that are true according to the reading.*

1. _____ There are fewer shy people now than there were in the past.

2. _____ Shy parents often have shy children.

3. _____ Most Israeli people are shy.

4. _____ Many shy people have older brothers and sisters.

5. _____ Children from big families often acquire social skills at home.

6. _____ Genetics, family size, and birthplace may all cause shyness.

7. _____ Shyness can cause serious problems.

8. _____ If you are shy now, you will be shy forever.

2. *Complete the outline of the reading. Don't look back at the reading.*

Topic: <u>Shyness</u>

   I. Shyness = common
      A. Almost 50% of people are shy

      B. _____% of people feel shy at some point

      C. These days shyness is becoming more common

      D. _____ are studying shyness

Main idea: Scientists have interesting _____ about why people are shy

  II. 1st idea about why people are shy = _____

      A. 15 to 20% of _____ behave shyly

      B. Shy babies usually have shy _____

  III. 2nd idea about why people are shy = _____

      A. Most shy children have _____ brothers/sisters

      B. Children with no brothers/sisters don't _____ social skills at home

  IV. 3rd idea about why people are shy = where you are _____

      A. In _____, most people say they are shy

      B. In _____, only one in three people say they are shy

      C. People in these countries have different opinions of _____

V. 4th idea about why people are shy = _____

    A. People who use the Internet lose practice at face-to-face _____

    B. Shyness has _____ by 10% in America in recent years

VI. Conclusion: For shy people, it can be difficult to make friends, _____ in class, get a good job

    A. Scientists say people can _____ their shyness

    B. They can practice conversation and try new things

3. *Now look back at the reading. Check your answers from Exercise 2. Correct any mistakes.*

B. A CLEANER WAY TO SHOP?

1. *Preview the newspaper article "A Cleaner Way to Shop?" Then answer the questions.*

1. What is the main idea of the reading?

    a. Online shopping costs more than shopping in a store.

    b. Online shopping is bad for the environment.

    c. You should not buy things online.

2. What helped you figure out the main idea?

    a. the picture

    b. the first sentence of the first paragraph

    c. the last sentence of the first paragraph

2. Read

Read "A Cleaner Way to Shop?" Underline the sentence that gives the main idea of the reading.

A CLEANER WAY TO SHOP?

Need to buy something? Why go to a store? Buy it on the Internet! Need it now? Why wait? Ask for next-day **delivery**! Each day, more and more people try online shopping. In fact, online sales have **doubled** in the last ten years. But,
5 not everyone is excited. Some scientists now say that online shopping is bad for the **environment**.

People are surprised to hear this. "They think, 'I don't need to drive, and the business doesn't need to build a store, so there will be less pollution,'" says Nuria Prost, an envi-
10 ronmental scientist. "But it is not so simple. In fact, online shopping is **wasteful**. It also adds to air pollution."

In truth, the Internet is not always as good a friend to the environment as it seems. For example, most people thought that computers would help offices use less paper and other **materials**. But paper use increased by 33 percent between
15 1986 and 1997. "[Online shopping] could have similarly negative effects," says Nevil Cohen, a professor of environmental science.

Part of the problem is what people are buying these days. In the past, people bought things on the Internet that did not **require** much packing material, such as books and clothing. But now people also shop online for large, heavy products such
20 as televisions, computers, and furniture. These products need to be packed in large amounts of plastic and paper. This creates a lot of waste.

Another problem caused by online shopping is air pollution. When **customers** buy products and ask for next-day delivery, companies often have to send them by air. Airplanes use much more **fuel** than cars and produce more carbon dioxide.[1]
25 When people buy a lot of different things from different online businesses, this creates even more travel by airplanes.

Online product returns are also a problem. For example, an online shoe store may **allow** customers to return shoes for free if they are the wrong size. This doubles the packing materials and number of airplane trips required to sell one
30 pair of shoes.

"If people want to protect the environment, they need to think before they shop," says Prost. "People need to ask themselves: Is this exactly what I want? Do I really need it tomorrow, or can I wait?" Online stores can also **charge** customers for returns. This may make people shop more carefully. "Online shopping is fast
35 and easy," says Prost, "but we can't forget the negative effect it has on the environment."

[1]**carbon dioxide:** the gas produced when people or animals breathe out or when carbon is burned in air, which may make the Earth warmer

3. Vocabulary Check

Write the boldfaced word from the reading next to the correct definition. Use the correct form of the word.

1. _____ = a substance such as coal, gas, or oil that can be burned to produce heat or energy

2. _____ = to need something

3. _____ = the act of bringing something (e.g., a letter or package) to a particular place or person

4. _____ = things such as wood, plastic, paper, etc., that are used for making or doing something

5. _____ = to give someone permission to do something

6. _____ = using more of something than is needed

7. _____ = someone who buys things from a store or company

8. _____ = the land, water, and air in which people, animals, and plants live

9. _____ = to become twice as large, or twice as much

10. _____ = to ask for a particular amount of money for a service or something you are selling

4. Read Again

Read "A Cleaner Way to Shop?" again and complete the comprehension exercises.

5. Comprehension Check

a. Read the statements about the reading. Write T (true) or F (false). If it is not possible to tell, write ?.

1. __T__ Online shopping is becoming more popular, but it is also wasteful.

2. _____ Most customers know that online shopping is bad for the environment.

3. _____ Most of the products customers buy online are big and weigh a lot.

4. _____ The delivery of heavy products requires a lot of materials.

5. _____ An airplane creates more pollution than a car.

6. _____ "Next day delivery" is helpful for the environment.

7. _____ When online stores charge a fee for returns, customers shop more carefully.

8. _____ Nuria Prost tells shoppers *not* to buy products on the Internet.

b. *Answer the questions. Try not to look back at the reading.*

1. What problem does online shopping cause?

_____

2. What are some reasons for the problem? List three.

_____

c. *Now look back at the reading. Check your answers from Exercise b. Correct any mistakes.*

Above material from: *Real Reading 2*

SKILL 4: MAKING INFERENCES

We make inferences all the time in our everyday lives. For example, suppose you see your friend. He has a cast on his leg, and he is walking with crutches. What inference can you make about your friend? You can infer that he hurt his leg.

An inference is an educated guess you make based on information you know, see, or read. Look at the three pictures following. The first person is watching TV. The second person is reading a book. The third person is watching a movie. Although we do not know the name of the TV show, book, or movie, we can make inferences about each one. We make the inferences based on the reaction of the person.

SKILL 4A: MAKING INFERENCES FROM PICTURES

Look at the pictures below and answer the questions.

1. What kind of show do you think the boy is watching? _____

    Why? _____

2. What kind of book do you think the girl is reading? _____

   Why? _____

3. What kind of movie do you think the woman is watching? _____

   Why? _____

SKILL 4B: MAKING INFERENCES FROM SENTENCES

Good readers make inferences when they read. Writers don't always tell you everything they want you to know. Sometimes they just give you hints and clues. They expect you to figure out some things on your own. In other words, they want you to make inferences.

An **inference** is an educated guess based on information in the reading. To make inferences you should combine the clues in the reading with information you already know from your own life.

Circle the letter of the inference you can make based on the information given.

Example

A boy goes into his house after walking home from school. He is carrying a wet umbrella.

  a. He washed his umbrella.

  ⓑ It is raining outside.

1. A young woman nervously opens a letter. She reads it quickly, smiles, starts jumping up and down, and yells, "Yes!"

  a. She received good news.

  b. She got a letter from her mother.

2. You hear car horns honking. Soon you hear tires screeching, a loud crash, and the sound of breaking glass.

   a. There was a car accident nearby.

   b. Someone threw glass bottles out of his car window.

3. A couple and their two children get into a taxi. They have several suitcases. The man is carrying a camera. They tell the taxi driver to take them to the airport.

   a. The man is a professional photographer.

   b. The family is going on a trip.

4. Two students are in the library. They are looking at their class notes. They have their history textbooks open.

   a. They are studying.

   b. They are on a date.

5. A young woman walked into work and proudly showed her coworkers her new diamond ring. Everyone was smiling. Some people were hugging her.

   a. The woman loves her job.

   b. The woman just got engaged.

6. Martha sent invitations to all her friends. She cleaned her house and bought flow-ers. She made lots of food and bought things to drink. She picked out her favorite CDs and put up some decorations.

   a. Martha is having a party.

   b. Martha is moving to a new apartment.

Read the following paragraphs and choose the best inference for each one. Circle the correct letter.

1.   Jack doesn't return Lillian's phone calls anymore. He also doesn't answer her e-mails. He walks on the other side of the street when he sees her coming. Her friends have tried to talk to him, but he ignores them.

   a. Jack doesn't like to use e-mail.

   b. Lillian's friends are angry with Jack.

   c. Jack is angry with Lillian.

2.   When Joanne got home from work she took two aspirin. She put on a sweater. Then she put on a coat. Then she turned the heat up in the apartment. When her sister Molly came home, she took Joanne's temperature and called the doctor.

   a. Joanne has a new sweater.

   b. Joanne is sick.

   c. Molly and the doctor are good friends.

3.　　　After the game, all the players on the team and their parents were hugging and kissing each other. It was a great day in the history of the team. The coach took them all out for ice cream to celebrate.

   a.　The team won the game.

   b.　It was the first game of the season.

   c.　Everyone on the team likes ice cream.

4.　　　Jennifer is changing her spending habits. She is eating at home more often instead of going to restaurants. She is getting books from the library instead of buying them. She is wearing the clothes she has and not shopping for new clothes.

   a.　Jennifer is trying to save money.

   b.　Jennifer likes old clothes.

   c.　Jennifer likes to cook.

Skill 4C: Making Inferences from Conversations

Work with a partner. Take the role of A and B and read the following conversations aloud. Then answer the inference questions that follow. Discuss why the others are wrong.

1.　A: Excuse me. I have to write a paper for my English class on the life of Agatha Christie. Can you help me find some information?
   B: I think you should start in the reference department with the computerized card catalog. Do you know how to use it?
   A: Yes, but where is the reference department?
   B: Just go up the stairs. It is the first room at the top of the stairs on your left. You'll see all the computers there and someone who can help you if you need it.

   1.　Where do you think the conversation is taking place?

   2.　What clues in the conversation helped you make your inference?

2.　A: Hurry up! We don't want to miss the beginning.
   B: I am hurrying! Why don't you get in line here to buy tickets, and I'll go inside and buy some popcorn.
   A: OK. I'll meet you at the food stand.
   B: If you see Ellen and Jake, ask them to save us two seats. They said they were coming too.
   A: OK, please get me a soda, too.
   B: Fine. I'll see you in a few minutes.

   1.　Where do you think the conversation is taking place?

   2.　What clues in the conversation helped you make your inference?

3.　A: How long has your tooth been hurting?
   B: Two weeks.
   A: Why didn't you come see me earlier?
   B: I thought it might get better. But, it's getting worse and worse.

A: Let me take a look. No wonder your tooth hurts. You have a big cavity. I'll fill it this week. Make an appointment with the receptionist.

B: Thanks.

1. Where do you think the conversation is taking place?

2. What clues in the conversation helped you make your inference?

4. A: Is everything OK here?

B: This is cold.

A: I'm sorry. I'll take it back to the kitchen for you and heat it up.

B: It's also too salty. What other soups do you have today?

A: Tomato, chicken with rice, and cream of mushroom.

B: Let me try the tomato soup.

A: I'll be right back with a new soup, sir.

1. Where do you think the conversation is taking place?

2. What clues in the conversation helped you make your inference?

5. A: Do you need some help?

B: Yes, do you have these in size 7?

A: I think so, but let me check. What color do you want?

B: Black.

A: Have a seat here and I'll be right back.

B: Please bring them in brown too. I can't decide!

A: Here you go. We have them in both colors.

B: These feel too small. My feet hurt when I walk.

A: Let me bring you size 7 1/2.

B: Thanks.

1. Where do you think the conversation is taking place?

2. What clues in the conversation helped you make your inference?

Above material from: *Get Ready to Read*

In these exercises, you will make inferences about the people in the conversations.

1. *Read the conversation. Make inferences to answer the questions. More than one answer may be possible.*

A: Do you think it'll be late?

B: Stop worrying, dear. It'll be just fine.

A: But look at all that rain and wind.

B: They didn't say anything when you checked in.

A: I know, but the weather's getting worse. Let's go ask again.

B: We don't need to. See, it says up there that your flight's on time.

A: I'm sorry, honey. You know I don't like flying! And I'm nervous about my meeting.

B: Why don't you take the train next time?

1. Where are these people? _____

2. Who are they? _____

3. What are they doing? _____

4. What can you infer about A? _____

5. What do you think will happen next? _____

2. *Talk about your answers with another student. Are they the same? What words helped you get your answers? Note: There may be more than one possible answer for many of the questions in these exercises. You should be ready to explain your answer.*

Explanation

1. They're at the airport, (*checked in, it says up there that your flight's on time*)

2. They're probably husband and wife. (*stop worrying, dear, honey*),

3. Waiting for A's flight. A is going away on a business trip. (*I don't like flying. And I'm nervous about my meeting.*)

4. She worries a lot. She's not very sure of herself.

5. Many answers are possible. For example:

   She will get on her flight and everything will be fine.

   Her flight will be delayed and she will miss her meeting.

   Her husband will get angry with her and they will have a fight.

3. *Read the conversation. Make inferences to answer the questions.*

A: Excuse me. Can you tell me what you think about this?
B: Hmm. Well, the color is perfect on you.
A: What about the style?
B: It's very popular. We sell a lot of those.
A: Does it look alright? It's so hard to find something that fits me right.
B: It looks great on you. It looks great on everyone.
A: You're sure it doesn't look a bit funny. I mean, the style's not too young for me?
B: No-o-o. You look very nice. Really.

1. Where are these people? _____

2. Who are they? _____

3. What are they doing? _____

4. What can you infer about A? _____

5. What can you infer about B? _____

6. What do you think will happen next? _____

Talk about your answers with another student. Are they the same? What words helped you get your answers?

4. *Read the conversation. Make inferences to answer the questions.*

A: I've got to tell you what happened yesterday.

B: What?

A: You know I had to stay late to finish that report? Well, I was here at my computer, and guess who came along . . . Sheila!

B: Sheila? You mean Sheila Gifford from the top floor?

A: That's right. She went right into Paul's office with a big pile of papers and stayed in there for about an hour.

B: You're kidding!

A: No, I'm serious. I could hear them talking. When she came out, she gave me a strange look. I thought she was going to say something, but she went straight to the elevator.

B: Oh, no. Do you think we've got bad news coming?

A: Well, if Sheila's in it, anything's possible.

1. Where are these people? _____

2. Who are they? _____

3. What are they talking about? _____

4. Who do you think Paul is? _____

5. How do the speakers feel about Sheila? _____

6. What do you think will happen next? _____

Talk about your answers with another student. Are they the same? What words helped you get your answers?

5. *Read the conversation. Make inferences to answer the questions.*

A: Hey you!

B: I'm sorry.

A: There's a stop sign!

B: I said I'm sorry . . .

A: You didn't even look!

B: I guess I wasn't thinking.

A: Yeah, I'll say. You know how much this is going to cost?

B: I don't know. It looks pretty bad.

A: I want all your info now. You know, registration, insurance, everything.

B: Jeez, what's my Dad going to say . . . ?

A: That's your problem. Come on. Let's get this done. I'm going to call the police, too. I don't want any trouble about this later.

1. Where are these people? _____

2. Who are they? _____

3. What are they talking about? _____

4. What can you infer about A? _____

5. What can you infer about B? _____

6. What do you think will happen next? _____

Talk about your answers with another student. Are they the same? What words helped you get your answers?

6. *Read the conversation. Make inferences to answer the questions.*

> A: Excuse me. Do you have the time?
> B: Nine o'clock.
> A: Already? Are you sure?
> B: Look, my watch says nine o'clock.
> A: Then, where's the Number 13?
> B: The Number 13? It's probably downtown by now.
> A: What do you mean?
> B: It probably came about fifteen minutes ago. It always comes at fifteen minutes before the hour.
> A: So, the next one isn't until nine forty-five?
> B: There's no next one. That was the last one.
> A: The last one?
> B: Yeah. After nine o'clock, there aren't any more.
> A: Oh, no! What's Trudy going to say! . . . But, wait a minute. What are you doing here?
> B: I'm waiting for a taxi . . . Where are you going? I'm going downtown, to Tremont Street. Are you heading that way? We could share.

1. Where are these people? _____

2. Who are they? _____

3. What are they talking about? _____

4. What can you infer about A? _____

5. What can you infer about B? _____

6. What do you think will happen next? _____

Talk about your answers with another student. Are they the same? What words helped you get your answers?

SKILL 4D: MAKING INFERENCES FROM STORIES

In each of these exercises, there is a passage from a book. You will try to infer more about the story from the information in the passage. There may be more than one possible answer for some questions.

Note: More than one answer is often possible in these exercises, too. You should be ready to explain your answers.

1. *Read the passage from* Anne of Green Gables, *by L. M. Montgomery. Make inferences to answer the questions. More than one answer may be possible.*

> When Anne woke up the next morning, she felt happy. She jumped out of bed and ran to the window.
>
> It was a beautiful morning. The sun shone and the sky was blue. Anne opened the window. Outside, there was a fruit tree with beautiful flowers. Anne could see
> 5 many other trees and flowers, and a small river, too.

"This is a wonderful place!" she thought. Then, suddenly, she remembered. She felt very sad again. "But, I can't stay here," she thought. "They don't want me because I'm not a boy."

Marilla came into the room. "Good morning Anne," she said. "Breakfast is 10 waiting. Wash your face and put on your clothes."

"I'm feeling very hungry," Anne said. "I can never be sad in the mornings. I love mornings."

After breakfast, Anne washed the plates and cups. Marilla watched carefully, but Anne did the job well.

15 "This afternoon I'm going to drive to White Sands," Marilla said. "You'll come with me, Anne, and we'll talk to Mrs. Spencer."

Matthew didn't say anything, but he looked very sad. Later, he got the horse and buggy ready for Marilla. Marilla drove, and Anne sat next to her.

"Is it a long way to White Sands?" asked Anne.

20 "About eight kilometers," answered Marilla. "I know you like to talk, Anne. So tell me your story."

"It isn't very interesting," said Anne. "I was born in Bolingbroke in Nova Scotia, and I was 11 last March. My parents were teachers. But, they died when I was a baby. So their cleaner, Mrs. Thomas, and her husband took me into their house.

25 "Mrs. Thomas had four children. I helped her with them. But then Mr. Thomas died in an accident. Mrs. Thomas and the children went to Mr. Thomas's parents. They didn't want me.

"Then Mrs. Hammond, Mrs. Thomas's friend, took me into her house. She had eight children. They were very hard work. Then Mrs. Hammond moved away. I had 30 to go to the orphanage because nobody wanted me. I was there for four months."

1. Where are these people? _____

2. Who are they? _____

3. When do you think this takes place? _____

4. What is happening? _____

5. How do the people probably feel? _____

6. What do you think will happen next? _____

7. What can you infer about Anne's personality? _____

2. *Read the passage from* Gentlehands, *by M.E. Kerr. Make inferences to answer the questions.*

I tried to convince Skye to let me drive to Beauregard with her that night and hitch a ride back to my house, but she wouldn't hear of it. She dropped me and took off like a rocket. I saw my father standing in our driveway by his Toyota, smoking a cigarette, watching me. He was in uniform because he was working nights that week.

5 "That was a Jensen she was driving," I said. "Did you ever hear of a Jensen?"

"Did she ever hear of a speed limit?"

"Oh, *Dad*."

"It isn't funny, Buddy," he said.

I stood there and he stood there, and then he said, "Where'd you go?"

10   I didn't want to tell him then. He wasn't in the greatest mood, and I didn't want to open that whole can of worms at the end of a beautiful evening.

"We just rode around."

"Rode around at eighty miles an hour?"

"She wasn't doing eighty."

15   "She was close to it," he said. He took a drag on his cigarette and twirled his car keys in his hand. "Buddy, if your social calendar isn't too full, I'd appreciate it if you'd do something with Streaker tomorrow."

"I work until two," I said.

"And after two?"

20   "I was going clamming[1] with Ollie."

"Take Streaker with you," he said. "Okay?"

"Okay," I agreed.

"Streaker hangs around his mother too much," my father said.

"I know that. Okay."

25   He gave me one of his friendly punches and opened his car door. "I've never even heard of a Jensen," he said.

"Neither had I," I said.

"Well, anyway, did you have a good time?"

"Yeah."

1. Where are these people? _____

2. Who are they? _____

3. How old do you think Buddy is? _____

4. Who do you think Streaker is? _____

5. What happened before this in the story? _____

6. What do you think will happen after this? _____

[1]**clamming** looking for clams at the seaside; *clams* are a kind of shellfish

Reprinted from *Gentlehands* by M. E. Kerr (1990), by permission of McIntosh & Otis, Inc. Copyright © 1978 by M. E. Kerr.

Talk about your answers with another student. Are they the same? What words helped you get your answers?

3. *Read the next part of the story from* Gentlehands. *Make inferences to answer the questions.*

She was all in blue, right down to her sandals. I guess she specialized in wearing all one color, and she had this great perfume on, and that smile, and she just stood there and I just stood there, and the jukebox was roaring out some rock number, and the whole place was babbling around us, waiters calling out: "Two over easy, 5 o.j., and one black."

"I came to get you," she said.

"I'm working," I said.

"I'm shopping," she said. "What time are you through working?"

"Two," I said.

10   "I'm going to take you for a swim," she said. "Would a swim make you happy, Buddy?"

"I guess it would," I said.

"Don't guess with me, Buddy," she said.

"BUDDY!" I could hear Kick behind me.

15   "Someone's calling you," she said. "I'll be parked outside at two sharp. Okay?"

"Okay," I said.

Before I'd left the house that morning, I'd stuck a note up in Streaker's bunk telling him to be ready at two thirty.

So much for promises, and clamming.

1. Where are the people? _____

2. What can you infer about Buddy after reading both passages? _____
   _____

3. What can you infer about his family? _____

4. What can you infer about the girl? _____

5. What is meant by "So much for promises, and clamming"? _____
   _____

6. What do you think will happen next? _____

Talk about your answers with another student. Are they the same? What words helped you get your answers?

Above material from: *Reading Power 2, Fourth Edition*

SKILL 4E: MAKING INFERENCES ABOUT PEOPLE

Read the following paragraphs and choose the best inference for each one.

1.   Sarah is a wonderful girl, but she is driving her mother crazy. Why? Because she talks constantly on her cell phone. Sarah thinks cell phones are the greatest invention of all time. She loves being able to stay in touch with all of her friends wherever she goes. However, Sarah's mother gets annoyed because she's tired of hearing the cell phone ring. She considers it an unwelcome interruption to family conversations. Now, she has given Sarah two rules. First, no answering the cell phone during dinnertime. Two, no using the cell phone while driving. It is very dangerous to drive and talk on a cell phone. Sarah has promised to follow these rules, and she tries not to use her cell phone too much when she is with her mother.

What can you infer from the paragraph?

a. Sarah's mother doesn't have a cell phone.

b. Sarah's mother doesn't think cell phones are the greatest invention in the world.

c. Sarah would rather talk on her cell phone than eat dinner with her family.

2.   Some people might complain about their jobs, but Janet never does. For three years, Janet has been a counselor at a state college. She helps hundreds of students choose and register for courses. Career counseling is her greatest interest. Janet enjoys finding websites about different occupations and helping students explore their options. Sometimes her day is very busy because lots of students come to the counseling office, especially at the beginning and end of each semester. Janet doesn't mind being busy, though. She loves working with people, giving advice, and finding solutions to problems.

What can you infer from the paragraph?

a. Janet is looking for a new job.

b. Janet likes her job.

c. Janet doesn't like her job.

3.   Once upon a time there was a king named Midas who had a large fortune but was never satisfied. No matter how many riches he had, he always wanted more. One day he saved the life of a magic fish. In return, the fish said that he would give Midas one wish. Midas thought about which wish would give him the greatest fortune. Then, he had his answer. Midas wished that everything he touched would turn to gold. First, Midas touched a flower and it turned to gold. Next, he touched a chair and it turned to gold. King Midas was very excited by his new ability to create enormous wealth. Suddenly, though, his daughter ran toward him. Midas had no time to stop her, and she, too, turned to gold. At that moment, Midas understood the true meaning of wealth and fortune.

What can you infer from the paragraph?

a. Midas realized that wealth and fortune are not always good things.

b. Midas realized that he wanted even more wealth and fortune.

c. Midas wanted to give his daughter wealth and fortune.

4.   Dave Thomas became a folk hero through his popular television commercials for Wendy's, the chain of fast-food restaurants he founded in 1969. He was always called "Dave" in the commercials, and was admired because of his honesty, good nature, and sense of humor. Wendy's, named after Dave's daughter, earned millions of dollars serving familiar fast foods such as hamburgers and fries, but also by offering other kinds of food such as baked potatoes, chili, and a variety of salads. The road to success wasn't always easy for Dave. He was adopted as an infant and dropped out of school at age fifteen. He considered dropping out of school to be his biggest mistake in life. After earning a fortune through Wendy's, Dave decided to finish high school. Dave devoted his later years to the Dave Thomas Foundation for Adoption, an organization he founded to increase awareness of adoption and make

the process more affordable. Dave died in 2002, and today he is remembered for his honesty and old-fashioned values.

What can you infer from the paragraph?

a. Dave believed that education was important.

b. Most people would rather eat chili than hamburgers.

c. Wendy's is the most popular fast-food chain in the United States.

5.   Rosa and Harry are looking for an apartment. They are going to get married next month, and they want to move into a nice place for their new home. However, finding an apartment isn't easy. Many of the apartments listed in the newspaper are too expensive, and the cheaper ones all have problems. The first apartment they looked at was too small, a studio with just one tiny room and a bathroom. The next apartment was very dirty and in bad condition. Everything seemed to be broken or falling apart. The third one was located on top of a restaurant and was too noisy. Rosa and Harry are going to look at another apartment tonight, and they hope that this one will be the perfect place.

What can you infer from the paragraph?

a. Rosa and Harry are too critical about the apartments they look at.

b. Rosa and Harry disagree about the kind of apartment they should rent.

c. Rosa and Harry are looking for a clean, quiet, moderately priced apartment.

SKILL 4F: MAKING INFERENCES FROM HISTORY

Work with a partner. Make an inference based on the information in each of the following paragraphs. Then, compare your inferences with the inferences of another pair of students.

1.   Catherine II was a German princess who became the empress of Russia in 1762. Catherine expanded Russia during her rule to include parts of the Ottoman Empire, Poland, and Siberia. In addition, she admired the culture of the West and encouraged interest in the arts, literature, science, and politics. She also built schools and hospitals, established the first school for girls, and gave women important political jobs. By the time of her death in 1796, she had turned Russia into a world power. For these reasons and for her success in modernizing the administration, she is remembered as Catherine the Great.

Inference: _____

2.   The world's population has been increasing at a fast rate during the past few centuries. Scientists estimate that for thousands of years, the human population grew slowly. After 1700, there was a steady increase in population because of better agricultural methods, improved sanitation, and advances in the field of medicine. The population has continued to grow at a fast pace. It took hundreds of thousands of years for the world's population to total about 1 billion in 1800. It reached 2 billion in just one more century and has rapidly grown to more than 7 billion today. Serious problems have resulted from this sudden population explosion. People are using up the world's natural resources at a faster rate than they can develop, forests are disappearing, and pollution is increasing. As the world's population continues to

increase sharply, these issues must be addressed for the safety and health of future generations.

Inference: _____

Above material from: *Ready to Read Now*

SKILL 4G: MAKING INFERENCES FROM A JOURNAL

You are going to read the journal that a young woman wrote as she traveled by train to the National Parks of the western United States.

As you read the journal, think about inferences you can make. Put a check next to the statements in the boxes that are logical inferences.

MY TRAVELS BY TRAIN IN THE WESTERN UNITED STATES

1   *Chris and Jan wanted to visit the western United States. They decided to take a **tour** on a train called the American Orient Express. The tour included all their food and transportation. They even slept on the train, so they didn't have to make any hotel reservations. Chris and Jan wanted to learn about the history, native people, plants, and animals of the western United States. They were happy that there was a **guide** on the tour to explain everything to them.*

Thursday, June 12

2   We flew to Salt Lake City, Utah, this morning and got on the train at 3:00 P.M. The train is beautiful, but our room is very small (very, very small!). First, we unpacked. Then, we went to the observation car to meet the other people on our tour. Everyone goes there to meet people and enjoy the **scenery** through its huge windows. The people on our tour seem very nice, and I'm sure we'll make lots of new friends. Tomorrow when we wake up, we'll go to Yellowstone National Park in Wyoming.

_____ Chris and Jan are not from the western United States.

_____ Chris and Jan wanted to meet people.

_____ Chris and Jan are sisters.

Friday, June 13

3   We got to Yellowstone at 10:00 this morning. We saw huge animals like buffalo, moose, bears, and elk, and smaller animals too. They are all **wild** and free and fun to watch. Of course we had to see Old Faithful, the most famous geyser in the world. Then, a group of us

decided to hike[1] a few miles up to a beautiful waterfall. I found some buffalo fur on the **trail**! It's silkier and softer than my cat's fur! I'm going to save it. We saw and learned so much today and had lots of fun with our new friends. Some people think Friday the 13th is an unlucky day, but it was a great day for us! When we got back to the train we were tired, but happy, and ready for a big dinner.

> _____ Chris believes Friday the 13th is an unlucky day.
>
> _____ Chris liked the buffalo fur.

Saturday, June 14

4 We woke up this morning at the Teton Mountains in western Wyoming. What an **amazing** sight! The Tetons are part of the Rocky Mountains. The highest point is called Grand Teton, and it is unforgettable. We only went up to 11,000 feet, but the air up there was thinner and colder than it was at the **bottom**. We hiked for miles on a beautiful trail with lots of pretty flow-  ers. The views of the mountains and lakes and wild animals were unbelievable. I will never forget how **gorgeous** the mountain scenery is here—especially because I took so many pictures! I probably took too many, but I couldn't stop until I ran out of film. By the time we got back on the train, I was exhausted from walking so much. But, I was ready for another big dinner after another great day of great new experiences with great new friends.

> _____ The Grand Teton is higher than 11,000 feet.
>
> _____ Chris took more pictures than Jan.

Sunday, June 15

5 We slept well as the train traveled to Utah and Zion National Park. No cars are allowed at Zion, so we walked or used the park bus to get around. Today was hotter than yesterday. It was 102 degrees Fahrenheit (38 degrees Centigrade). Our guide told us to bring **at least** a half-gallon of water to drink! We stayed at the bottom of the canyon and hiked along the river there. The view is amazing from the bottom. When I looked up at the rocks, I felt very small. They rise 3,000 feet (914 meters) toward the sky. Wind and water have changed the rocks into unusual shapes. Our guide said, "Nature is an amazing machine," and he was right. Jan pointed to two people climbing up the side of a rock. That looked **scary**. They were so high that it was hard to see them.

[1]**hike**: to take a long walk in the country or mountains

Monday, June 16

6   Today, Arizona: The Grand Can-
yon! Our guide pointed out that the
Grand Canyon is not the widest, longest, or deepest canyon in the world,
but it is the grandest. We hiked along
an easy trail. I stayed on the trail, but
Jan went off the trail to take pictures.
She got very close to the edge. I told
her it was unsafe, but I'm sure her
pictures will be wonderful. Lots of
people go by mule or on foot down to
the bottom of the canyon. Not me, of course. Too scary! The Grand Canyon is a special
place for Native Americans like the Hopi and the Navajo. They lived in the canyon a
thousand years ago, and the land is still important to them. Today, they only go there
for religious purposes. There is a lot to learn about the land and people of this area.

Tuesday, June 17

7   This morning we woke up in Albuquerque, New
Mexico. After our usual big breakfast, we went to
Bandelier National Monument. This is one of the
places where the Anasazi Indians once lived. They
made their homes in caves on the sides of high rock
cliffs. How did they do that? It's not easy to get up to
those caves. Our guide told us that the Anasazi first
moved to this canyon in the late 1100s and stayed for
about 400 years. The park has trails and ladders to
make it easier for tourists to see inside some of the
caves. I decided to be brave and climb up a 10-foot
ladder to see inside a cave. I got to see the pictures
the Anasazi drew on the walls so long ago. They were
very interesting. Naturally, Jan wanted to climb up to
the highest cave—180 feet (55 meters) up! She's a lot
braver than I am. Of course, I **would rather** stay on the ground and worry. Tonight
was our farewell dinner. It was sad to say goodbye to these special friends after
traveling so far with them. We all got along so well together. This was the most
wonderful trip I've ever taken.

> _____ Chris is afraid of heights.
>
> _____ Jan is not afraid of heights.
>
> _____ The Anasazi drew pictures of animals on the walls
> of the caves.

Cultures of the World

WRITING 1

Writing to communicate dates back thousands of years. Writing started as symbols on a cave wall, and then, about 3,500 years ago, people began to use alphabets.

Different languages use different writing systems.

Different languages also use different writing styles of organization. **English** organization, for example, is fairly simple. English uses a straight line from beginning to end. For instance, when English speakers read an article, they expect the article to have a beginning, a middle, and an end. The beginning should say what the article is going to be about, the middle should talk about the topic of the article, and the end should say what the article was about. Here is a diagram of the English style of writing.[1]

[1]**Source:** Based on Kaplan, R.B. "Cultural thought patterns in intercultural education." *Language Learning*, 16 (1), 1966.

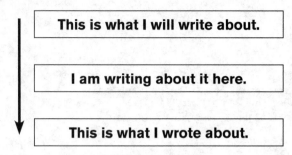

Diagram 1: English Organization

In this book, you will learn the American English Style of Writing.

Above material from: *Writing to Communicate 2, Third Edition*

THE WRITING PROCESS

Very few people pick up a pen or sit down at a computer and produce a perfect piece of writing on the first try. Most writers spend a lot of time thinking before they write and then work through a series of steps while they are composing. The final product is often the result of several careful *revisions*. It takes patience as well as skill to write well. You should think of writing as a process involving the following steps:

Step One: Prewriting
generating ideas, planning, and organizing your ideas

↓

Step Two: Writing
using your ideas to write a first draft

↓

Step Three: Revising and Editing
improving what you have written

In this unit you will learn more about these three steps.

A. STEP ONE: PREWRITING

For many people, the hardest part of writing is *getting started*. Whether you enjoy writing or not, you will find it easier to write if you do some prewriting exercises to get started. Prewriting is a way to warm up your brain before you write, just as you warm up your car's engine before you drive.

1. Generating Ideas

Writers use a variety of prewriting techniques to generate ideas. Two of the most popular are *brainstorming* and *clustering*.

"Sometimes you get a brainstorm, sometimes you just get the clouds."

Courtesy of Randy Glasbergen. Copyright © Randy Glasbergen/Glasbergen.com.

Brainstorming

Brainstorming is a quick way to generate a lot of ideas on a subject. The purpose is to come up with a list of as many ideas as possible without worrying about how you will use them. Your list may include words, phrases, sentences, or even questions. To brainstorm, follow these steps:

1. Begin with a broad topic.

2. Write down as many associations as you can in ten minutes.

3. Add more items to your list by answering the questions: *What? How? When? Where? Why?* and *Who?*

4. Group the items on the list that go together.

5. Cross out items that do not belong.

Your list may seem very unfocused as you are working on it. But, you will later go back and organize the items on your list and decide which ones you want to include in your essay and which you want to discard.

Look at the list of ideas a student wrote when she brainstormed about the general topic of superstitions.

Topic: Superstitions
my sister is very superstitious
breaking a mirror
look for four-leaf clovers
superstitions in different countries
sit in center of room for tests
finding a penny
origin of superstitions

Friday the 13th

always wear pearl necklace for tests

don't stay on 13th floor in a hotel

wear lucky T-shirt for games

wedding superstitions

eat scrambled eggs for breakfast on day of a game

don't step on cracks

don't walk under ladders

animal superstitions

wear green when I fly

use lucky shoelaces in tennis shoes

never start a trip on Friday

switch watch to right wrist for tests

After the student made her list, she read it over and decided to write an essay that focused on her personal superstitions. Then she crossed out items on the list that did not relate to the focus.

Topic: Superstitions

~~my sister is very superstitious~~

breaking a mirror

look for four-leaf clovers

~~superstitions in different countries~~

sit in center of room for tests

finding a penny

~~origin of superstitions~~

Friday the 13th

always wear pearl necklace for tests

don't stay on 13th floor in a hotel

wear lucky T-shirt for games

~~wedding superstitions~~

eat scrambled eggs for breakfast on day of a game

don't step on cracks

don't walk under ladders

~~animal superstitions~~

wear green when I fly

use lucky shoelaces in tennis shoes

never start a trip on Friday

switch watch to right wrist for tests

Next, she organized her ideas into three categories of her personal superstitions: tests, travel, and sports.

Tests

always wear pearl necklace for tests

sit in center of room for tests

switch watch to right wrist for tests

Travel

never start a trip on Friday

don't stay on 13th floor in a hotel

wear green when I fly

Sports

wear lucky T-shirt for games

use lucky shoelaces in tennis shoes

eat scrambled eggs for breakfast on day of a game

Practicing Brainstorming

In the space below, brainstorm a list of ideas for the general topic of travel.

_____

_____

_____

_____

_____

_____

_____

_____

_____

Now, look at your list and choose a focus for a paragraph you could write. Cross out any items that do not relate to that focus. Finally, group similar ideas together.

_____

_____

_____

_____

_____

_____

_____

_____

_____

Clustering

Clustering is a visual way of generating ideas. If you prefer to work with information visually, clustering might be a good technique for you. It shows the connections among your ideas using circles and lines. To cluster, follow these steps:

1. Write your topic in the center of a piece of paper and draw a circle around it.

2. Think about your topic and write any ideas that come to mind in circles around the main circle.

3. Connect these ideas to the center circle with lines.

4. Think about each of your new ideas, write more related ideas in circles around them, and connect them to their corresponding ideas with a line.

5. Repeat this process until you run out of ideas.

The following is an example of a cluster diagram one student made on the topic of *communication*. In this example, what topic or topics would he probably choose to write about? Why?

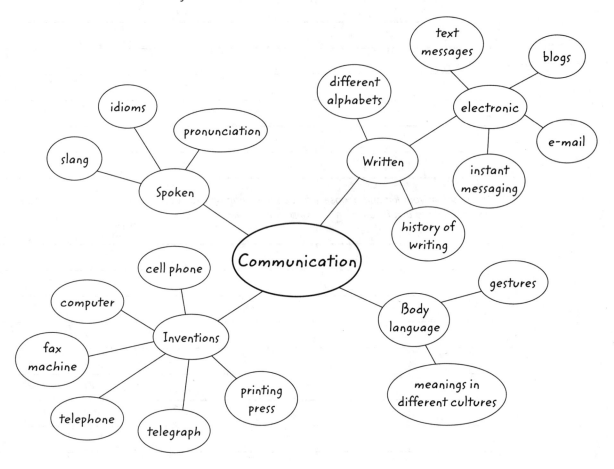

Unit Three   Above material from: *Ready to Write 3, Third Edition*

B. The Parts of a Three-Paragraph Process Essay

The three-paragraph essay has three parts: an introduction, a body paragraph, and a conclusion. The following outline tells you what you should put into each part of your essay.

I.   Introduction
  A. Gains the reader's attention
  B. Introduces the topic
  C. States the writer's thesis

II. Body paragraph
  A. Begins with a topic sentence that tells how many steps there are in the process
  B. Includes supporting details, explanation, and examples

III. Conclusion
  A. Restates the thesis
  B. Summarizes the major points
  C. Gives the reader something to think about

Above material from: *ELS Language Centers*

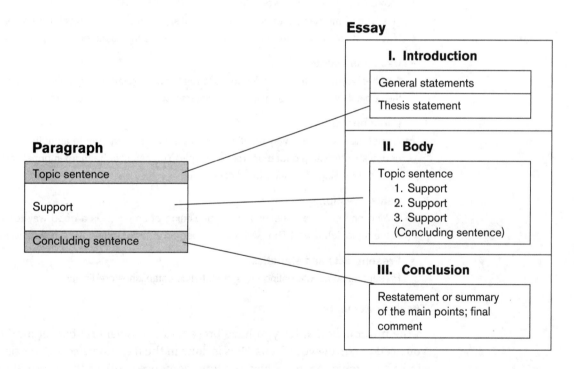

An essay **introduction** consists of two parts: a few general statements to attract your reader's attention and a **thesis statement** to state the main idea of the essay. A thesis statement for an essay is like a topic sentence for a paragraph: It names the specific topic and gives the reader a general idea of the contents of the essay. The **body** consists of one paragraph. The paragraph develops the topic. The **conclusion**, like the concluding sentence in a paragraph, is a summary or review of the main points discussed in the body.

An essay has **unity** and **coherence**, just as a paragraph does. **Transition signals** and the **repetition of key nouns** link the paragraphs into a cohesive whole.

C. WRITING: A THREE PARAGRAPH ESSAY

1. The Introduction

The *introduction* is the first paragraph of your essay. It should capture the reader's attention and create a desire to read the rest of the essay. The introduction should start with a general discussion of your subject and lead up to a specific statement of your main idea, or thesis.

The format of an introductory paragraph is different from the format of most other kinds of paragraphs. In introductory paragraphs, the main idea is usually stated in the *last* sentence. This sentence is called the *thesis statement*.

The function of the introduction is:

- to capture the reader's interest.
- to provide background information.
- to state the main idea of the essay in a thesis statement.

There are no specific rules for writing an introduction, but there are several techniques. Many introductions use one or a combination of the following techniques to provide background information and capture the reader's attention.

- **Move from general to specific.**
  This type of introduction opens with a general statement on the subject that establishes its importance and then leads the reader to the more specific thesis statement.

- **Use an anecdote.**
  Another way to write an introduction is to relate an interesting story that will interest the reader in the subject. Newspaper and magazine writers frequently use this technique to begin their articles.

- **Use a quotation.**
  A quotation is an easy way to introduce your topic. You can quote an authority on your subject or use an interesting quotation from an article. You can also be more informal and use a proverb or favorite saying of a friend or relative.

- **Ask a question.**
  Asking one or more questions at the beginning of an essay is a good way to engage readers in the topic right away. They will want to read on in order to find the answers to the questions.

- **Present facts and statistics.**
  Presenting some interesting facts or statistics establishes credibility.

Thesis Statements

In the introduction, after you have presented some general background information, you need to narrow your focus. This is done in the *thesis statement*. A thesis statement is similar to a topic sentence. Just as a topic sentence controls the information for a paragraph, a thesis statement controls the information for an entire essay.

The thesis statement is a sentence that tells the reader what the essay will be about and what points you will make in the essay. Your thesis statement should state the subject of the essay, explain your purpose, and list the main supporting ideas from your outline.

A good thesis statement:

- identifies the subject of the essay.
- states the purpose of the essay.
- tells the focus of the subject.

2. The Body (Supporting Paragraph)

The body of a three-paragraph essay consists of a supporting paragraph that supports the thesis. A supporting paragraph develops the point about the subject. The paragraph begins with a topic sentence that is supported with specific details, facts, and examples.

3. The Conclusion

The final paragraph of your essay is the *conclusion*. It is the last thing your readers will see, so you want to make it interesting.

The purpose of this last paragraph is to summarize, without using the same words, the main point you have made in your essay. Your concluding paragraph should also leave your reader agreeing, disagreeing, or at least thinking about your thesis.

The purpose of the conclusion is to:

- restate the thesis
- summarize the main ideas
- leave your reader with something to think about.

There are no specific rules for writing a conclusion, but there are several techniques you can use. Many conclusions use one or a combination of the following techniques to wrap up the essay.

- **Restate your main point.**

  When you use this method of finishing your essay, you restate the main point you presented in your essay. Make sure that you do not repeat your exact words. Try to figure out a new way to say it.

- **Ask a question.**

  When you ask a provocative question, it will keep the readers thinking about the topic.

- **Suggest a solution; make a recommendation or prediction.**

  Depending on the topic of your essay, the conclusion might be a good place for you to suggest a solution to a problem that you have discussed, or to make a recommendation or a prediction.

4. Essay Plan: Process

Use the following plan as a guide when you write a three-paragraph process essay.

Process Essay Plan

Introduction
1. State what the process is and why it is important.
2. Define the process.
3. State the purpose for explaining the process.
4. List any equipment, ingredients, or supplies needed to perform the process.
5. Write a thesis statement that states the topic and explains that a series of steps is required.

Supporting Paragraph
1. Include a topic sentence for the supporting paragraph that states the main steps and their purpose.
2. Describe the steps in the process, using time order.
3. If there are a lot of steps, group them into several main stages.

---

continued

Conclusion

1. Review why the process is important.
2. Summarize the main steps in the process without the details.

Keep your audience in mind while you are writing a process essay. Ask yourself, "What do my readers know about my topic?" This will help you decide what steps and terms need more or less explanation.

D. WRITING A PROCESS ESSAY

In this activity, you will practice writing an essay that describes the steps in a process.

1. Prewriting

a. *Choose one of the topics below or your own topic to write about. Make a list of steps in the process on the lines that follow.*

How to . . .
- wash a car
- make rice, tea, a salad, noodles, etc.
- write a good paragraph or essay
- study for an exam
- annoy your teacher, your boss, or your parents
- make a paper airplane, knit a scarf, paint a picture, etc.

_____

_____

_____

_____

_____

_____

_____

_____

b. *Organize the steps according to time order. Prepare an informal outline.*

Topic: How to _____

_____

_____

_____

_____

_____

_____

2. Writing

Now write your process essay.

THE LANGUAGE OF PROCESS: USEFUL PHRASES AND SENTENCE PATTERNS

Process essays are organized according to time. When you write a process essay, you should begin by describing the first step in the process and continue in time until you have described the last step in the process. Transition words help the reader understand the sequence of the steps. Some common transitional words used in process essays are listed below.

TRANSITION SIGNALS THAT INDICATE THE ORDER OF STEPS IN A PROCESS		
first	soon afterward	every time
the first step	the third step	whenever
from then on	then	meanwhile
next	at this point	while
the next step	as	during
before	as soon as	the last step
after	when	finally
after that		

1. *Complete the paragraph with words and phrases from the chart.*

Do you avoid parking on busy streets because you are not good at parallel parking? Believe it or not, parallel parking is not as difficult as you think, especially if you follow these steps. _____, find a parking spot that is big enough for your car. _____, use your turn signal to let other drivers know that you are going to park. _____, pull ahead of the spot until you are next to the car parked in front of the spot. Your rear bumper should be even with that car's rear bumper. _____, put the car in reverse and start backing up slowly. _____ the car starts moving, turn the wheel as far as it will go toward the curb and back slowly and carefully into the space. _____ your front door is even with the rear bumper of the car in front of you, begin turning the steering wheel in the opposite direction—away from the curb. Continue to turn the steering wheel away from the curb as you slowly back into the space. _____, straighten out the steering wheel and drive forward or back in the space until your car is centered between the car in front of you and the one behind you.

2. *The following sentence patterns are useful in writing thesis statements for process essays:*

1. **It is** {easy / simple / not difficult} **to** _____ **if you have the right** {tools. / equipment. / materials. / ingredients.}

It is *easy* **to** *change a flat tire* **if you have the right** *equipment.*

It is *easy* **to** *build a platform bed* **if you have the right** *materials.*

It is *not difficult* **to** *make a cheese soufflé* **if you have the right** *ingredients.*

2. _____ **is easy when you follow** {these steps. / these directions. / these instructions. / this procedure.}

Making a delicious omelet **is easy when you follow** *these steps.*

Impressing your boss **is easy when you follow** *these instructions.*

Parallel parking **is easy if you follow** *these directions.*

3. **There are** {three / four / several} **major steps involved in** _____.

There are *three* **major steps involved in** *studying for an exam.*

There are *several* **steps involved in** *growing a vegetable garden.*

There are *several* **steps involved in** *writing a good paragraph.*

Write a thesis statement for a process essay on each of the essay topics below. Use a variety of sentence patterns.

1. **Topic:** How to write an essay

Thesis Statement: <u>*Writing a good essay is easier if you follow three main steps.*</u>

2. **Topic:** How to impress your teacher or boss

Thesis Statement: _____

_____

3. **Topic:** How to stay in shape

Thesis Statement: _____

_____

4. **Topic:** How to make a pizza

Thesis Statement: _____

_____

5. **Topic:** How to build a tree house

Thesis Statement: _____

_____

6. **Topic:** The best way to lose weight

   Thesis Statement: _____

   _____

7. **Topic:** How to make a beautiful flower arrangement

   Thesis Statement: _____

   _____

8. **Topic:** How to decorate your dorm room

   Thesis Statement: _____

   _____

9. **Topic:** How to pack for a weekend trip

   Thesis Statement: _____

   _____

10. **Topic:** How to quit smoking

    Thesis Statement: _____

    _____

11. **Topic:** How to network for a new job

    Thesis Statement: _____

    _____

12. **Topic:** How to relax after a stressful day at work or school

    Thesis Statement: _____

    _____

13. **Topic:** How to make new friends

    Thesis Statement: _____

    _____

Above material from: *Ready to Write 3, Third Edition*

READING 1

A. *Read the model essay, "How to Cook a Superior Steak" and answer the following questions.*

1. Underline the thesis statement.

2. What technique does the author use in the introduction to capture your attention?

   a. Move from general to specific

   b. Use an anecdote

   c. Use a quotation

    d. Ask a question

    e. Present facts and statistics

3. How many steps are involved in the process?

4. Circle the transition signals

5. Does the author restate the thesis in the conclusion?

6. Does the author summarize the main ideas of the body paragraph?

Above material from: ELS Language Centers

MODEL ESSAYS

Model Essay 1

HOW TO COOK A SUPERIOR STEAK

My girlfriend Alicia loves meat. While other women choose raw vegetables and nonfat yogurt, she orders a huge steak every time we go out. Because these restaurant meals were getting pretty expensive, I decided to learn to cook her favorite food at home. Cooking an excellent steak is easy if you follow these five steps.

First, you should do your shopping carefully. A cooked steak is only as good as the cut of meat you select. Choose the best cut you can afford. Second, when you get the steak home, measure the thickness. The third step is to heat the grill so that it is extremely hot. Then, put the steak on the very hot grill and immediately turn it over to brown it on both sides. Since Alicia likes her steak very pink in the center, I have learned to cook her steak no more than ten minutes per inch of thickness. This locks in the juices and makes it tender. Finally, never answer the telephone while cooking steak because it can easily get overcooked. A rare steak is best, and Alicia won't have it any other way.

What About You?
Do you like to eat meat? If so, is this how you cook it? If not, what is your favorite food to cook?

Since Alicia doesn't cook, she doesn't know how easy this meal is. She thinks I am a great chef! If you follow these directions, you can make someone happy, too. Enjoy eating your delicious steak!

Above material from: Writing to Communicate, Second Edition

B. *Read the process essay, "How to Gain Fifty Pounds," and answer the following questions.*

1. Underline the thesis statement.

2. What technique does the author use in the introduction to capture your attention?

    a. Move from general to specific.

    b. Use an anecdote.

    c. Use a quotation.

   d. Ask a question.

   e. Present facts and statistics.

3. What is the topic sentence of the first body paragraph?

4. What two general steps does the author recommend to gain weight? Identify two supporting details for each step.

5. Does the author restate the thesis?

Above material from: *ELS Language Centers*

Model Essay 2

HOW TO GAIN FIFTY POUNDS

When we are born, we all weigh between six and ten pounds. Nevertheless, as we grow, some of us increase to 300 pounds and some of us only to 100 pounds. Why does this happen? Part of it has to do with genetics and whether our genes tell us to grow tall and big or short and slim. On the other hand, a large part of the difference also has to do with our habits. It's not difficult to gain weight if you follow these steps.

You only need two ingredients to gain weight: less activity and more food. The body is a rather simple machine. It takes in fuel in the form of food, and it burns fuel through exercise. If the body takes in more fuel from the calories in food than it burns off in living and exercising, it will store the extra calories as body fat.

The first step in the process of gaining weight is to decrease your daily level of activities. For example, if you usually walk to work or school, you can drive instead. Make sure you park very close to your workplace so you don't have to move much, and take the elevator instead of the stairs. If you usually enjoy a game of tennis or like to jog, stop! Remember that aerobic exercise is your enemy. Every way you can find to decrease the amount of calories you burn will help you add more pounds. Secondly, you need to consume as many calories as you can. If you usually eat a lot of vegetables or fruits, that makes it hard. In order to gain weight, you need the kind of food that has a large amount of calories per gram. For that reason, if you eat a doughnut or three for breakfast instead of a bowl of cereal with milk, you'll be sure to gain weight. Similarly, if you substitute a double cheeseburger for your normal lunchtime apple and yogurt, you'll gain even more. Finally, make sure to drink a lot of sugary soft drinks with your meal.

As you can see, gaining weight is easy. You may not like all that fat and sugar in the beginning, but if you work at it, you'll get quite used to it. By following these steps, I promise you can gain fifty pounds in a year.

Above material from: *Writing to Communicate 2, Third Edition*

C. Meet Lesmor. Lesmor is an international student in a reading and writing class. She has written a process paragraph, and is working on expanding it into a three-paragraph process essay.

Read Lesmor's process paragraph and answer the following questions.

1. What process is the student describing?

2. What is the topic sentence of the paragraph?

3. How many steps are involved in the process?

4. What transition words are used?

5. What is the concluding sentence?

PROCESS PARAGRAPH: HOW TO CLEAN UP AFTER A PARTY

Cleaning up after a party is easy if you follow a few simple steps. First, gather some supplies, such as trash bags, furniture polish, paper towels, and a vacuum cleaner. It also doesn't hurt to ask a few friends for help! Second, pick up any trash and recycle any bottles and cans. Next, open the windows to let in the fresh air. Take down the decorations and put away any leftover food. After that, straighten the pictures and put the furniture back where it belongs. Finally, clean the tables with furniture polish and vacuum the floor. Now, you can relax!

Notice how she has taken the information from her paragraph to complete the outline for her essay. She has also added sentences to develop her introductory and concluding paragraphs.

I. Introduction
   A. Topic Sentence: Most people love parties.
   B. Thesis: Cleaning up after a party is easy if you follow a few simple steps.

II. Body Paragraph
   A. Topic sentence: After a party, the process of cleaning up your home is easy.
   B. Details
      1. Gather supplies
      2. Ask friends

3. Trash and recycling
4. Open windows
5. Decorations and food
6. Pictures and furniture
7. Clean tables and vacuum
   C. Concluding sentence: Now your home is clean and you can relax!

III. Conclusion
   A. Restatement of thesis: In conclusion, cleaning up after a party is simple when you follow this process.
   B. Concluding sentence: The next time you have a party, you can enjoy yourself because cleaning up is easy!

Now, read the essay Lesmor has created from her paragraph and answer the following questions.

1. What is the thesis of the essay?

2. What is the topic sentence of the body paragraph?

3. Does the author restate her thesis in the conclusion? Does she summarize the points from the body paragraph?

PROCESS ESSAY: HOW TO CLEAN UP AFTER A PARTY

Most people love parties. We love to spend time with our friends and have fun. However, if you have the party at your house, you will need to clean up afterwards. This can be a difficult job, but don't worry! Cleaning up from a party is easy if you follow a few simple steps.

After a party, the process of cleaning up your home is easy. First, gather a few supplies. You will need some trash bags, furniture polish, paper towels, and a vacuum cleaner. It also doesn't hurt to ask a few friends for help! Second, pick up any trash and recycle all bottles and cans. Next, open the windows to let in the fresh air. Take down the decorations and put away any leftover food. After that, straighten the pictures and put the furniture back where it belongs. Finally, clean the tables with furniture polish and paper towels, and vacuum the floor. Now, your home is clean and you can relax!

In conclusion, cleaning up after a party is simple when you follow this process. It just involves getting the correct supplies and doing a little bit of work. The next time you have a party, you can enjoy yourself because cleaning up is easy!

Above material from: ELS Language Centers

WRITING 2

WRITE YOUR OWN PROCESS ESSAY

Now choose one of the topics below and write your own process essay.

Topic Suggestions: How to
Get an A in English
Get an F in English
Learn a new language
Change a flat tire
Study for a test
Catch a fish

Make pizza/baklava/borscht/nachos (or any special food)
Make a piñata
Use chopsticks
Play a children's game
Heal a broken heart
Get a boyfriend/girlfriend
Get a U.S. driver's license
Clean your room
Do laundry
Get a good night's sleep
Turn your friends into enemies
Make coffee/tea

Now use the following template to create your outline for your essay.

I. Introduction _____

   A. Capture the reader's attention _____

   _____

   B. Provide background information _____

   _____

   C. Thesis _____

   _____

II. Body paragraph

   A. Topic sentence _____

   _____

   B. Supporting details _____

   _____

   C. Concluding sentence _____

   _____

III. Conclusion

   A. Restate the thesis _____

   _____

   B. Summarize the main ideas _____

   _____

   C. Leave the reader with something to think about _____

   _____

READING 2

PROCESS READING MODELS

FIRST READING

A. BEFORE YOU READ

Answer these questions.

1. What is a mummy?

2. Which countries have mummies?

3. Where can you see mummies today?

B. READING

HOW DID THE EGYPTIANS MAKE MUMMIES?

1   The ancient Egyptians **believed** in many gods. They also believed that their kings, called pharaohs, were gods. They believed that the pharaoh could help them even after he died. Because of this, they wanted the pharaoh to have a good life, and a good life after death, or afterlife. One way to give the pharaoh a good afterlife was to **preserve** his body. Egyptians believed this was important for the pharoah's **spirit**. This would help the spirit **recognize** the body. This is the reason the Egyptians made mummies.

2   As soon as a pharaoh died, the top priest, together with his helpers, started work on the body. They took out some of the organs but left the heart inside the body. They dried the organs and put them in special jars. Later they put the jars in the pharaoh's tomb, a special building for the dead. Next they took out the brain and threw it away. The Egyptians did not think the brain was important. On the outside of the body, they rubbed a kind of salt on the skin to help dry the body completely. This took about forty days. Then they filled the body with cloth and sand to keep its shape, rubbed it with oil and perfumes, and covered it with lots of **wax**. The Arabic word for wax is *mum*, so that's how we got the word *mummy*.

3   The pharaoh's body was now prepared. Next they wrapped it in very long pieces of cloth. Again, they used a lot of wax to make the pieces stick together. **At last**, after seventy days, the mummy was ready. They painted the face of the dead pharaoh on the mummy to help his spirit recognize him. The mummy then went into two or three coffins, one inside the other, and finally into the tomb.

4   During his lifetime, a pharaoh also prepared for the afterlife. He built his tomb, which took many years and a lot of hard work. The tomb was **in the shape of** a pyramid. The pointed top helped the pharaoh's spirit climb into the sky to join the gods who lived there. Each pharaoh tried to be greater than the one before, so the pyramids got larger and larger. More than seventy pharaohs built pyramids

for themselves. The Great Pyramid at Giza is still the largest stone structure in the world. The tomb was filled with everything the person needed for the afterlife, **such as** food, clothing, and jewelry. There were also model figures of men and women called *shabtis*. These figures became workers for the pharaoh in the afterlife. Some tombs had 365 shabtis, one for each day of the year.

5   Later other people such as priests, people in government, and rich Egyptians also wanted to be mummies so that they could join the pharaoh in the afterlife. They even made some animals such as cats, dogs, and birds into mummies because these animals represented gods.

6   When everything was in the tomb, they closed it very **tight**. Egyptians believed a pharaoh's tomb was like the house of a god. If someone entered it, terrible things would happen to that person—he or she could even die. But this did not stop people from entering the tombs. During construction, some workers built secret **tunnels** into the pyramids. Then, they went in later to **steal** from them. Some coffins had special doors for the same reason. **Thieves** went into almost all the tombs. They stole **treasures** such as gold and jewelry.

7   Today, most of the treasures are lost or in museums, but the pyramids of Egypt are still there. Every year, thousands of tourists from around the world visit the pyramids and think of the pharaohs who built them. So in a way, the pharaohs reached their goal—they live on, at least through their tombs.

C. Vocabulary

1. Meaning

Write the correct words in the blanks.

recognize	preserve	steal	treasures	wax
thieves	tunnels	tight	spirit	

1. Egyptians wanted to keep the body of the pharaoh in good condition after he died. They wanted to _____ the body.

2. The Egyptians believed that after a person died, his or her _____ was still alive.

3. The Egyptians used _____, a sticky substance made by bees, to make a mummy.

4. They painted the face of the dead person on the mummy to help his spirit _____ him.

5. They put everything in the tomb and closed it _____. They wanted the tombs to stay shut.

6. The tombs had _____ in them like gold and jewelry.

7. Some people wanted the gold and jewelry. They went into the tomb to _____ them.

8. _____ took gold and jewelry from the tombs.

9. They dug through the pyramids to make special roads and passages called _____.

2. Words That Go Together

Write the correct words in the blanks.

believed in	at last	in the shape of	such as

1. The ancient Egyptians _____ many gods.

2. The pharaohs wanted their tombs to look like pyramids. They built the tombs _____ pyramids.

3. It took a long time to clean, dry, and wrap the dead body. _____, after seventy days, the mummy was ready.

4. The Egyptians did many things to the dead body, _____ filling it with sand, rubbing it with oil, and covering it with wax.

3. Use

Work with a partner to answer the questions. Use complete sentences.

1. What do we use *wax* for today?

2. How can you *preserve* food?

3. Where do we usually find *tunnels*?

4. How do you *recognize* your house or apartment from the others near it?

5. Do you have any *treasures*? What are they?

6. What kinds of jewelry do you like? Give examples with *such as*.

7. Did someone ever *steal* something from you? What was it?

D. COMPREHENSION

1. Understanding the Reading

Circle the letter of the correct answer.

1. The ancient Egyptians believed in _____.

   a. pharaohs

   b. life after death

   c. mummies

   d. tombs

2. Workers started to build a tomb for a pharaoh _____.

   a. during the pharaohs lifetime

   b. after the pharaoh died

   c. when the pharaoh was old

   d. when a pharaoh was born

3. Thieves stole the _____ from most of the pyramids in Egypt.

    a. mummies

    b. treasures

    c. tombs

    d. shabtis

2. Remembering Details

Reread the passage and answer the questions.

1. Who usually made the pharaoh's mummy?

2. What organ did they leave in the body?

3. Where did they put the special jars with the organs in them?

4. How long did it take to make a mummy?

5. Why was the tomb of a pharaoh in the shape of a pyramid?

6. How many pharaohs built pyramids?

7. Why did they put *shabtis* in the tomb?

3. Making Inferences

All of the statements below are true. Some of them are stated directly in the reading. Others can be inferred, or guessed, from the reading. Write S for each stated fact. Write I for each inference.

1. ____ When an ordinary woman died, they did not make her into a mummy.

2. ____ The top priest and his helpers made the pharaoh's mummy.

3. ____ The tomb was in the shape of a pyramid so the pharoah's spirit could climb to the gods in the sky.

4. ____ The Egyptians thought the heart was a very important organ.

5. ____ A cat or dog was higher than an ordinary person.

4. Tell the Story

Work with a partner or together as a class. Tell the story of how the ancient Egyptians made mummies. Use your own words. Your partner or other students can ask questions about the story.

5. Discussion

Discuss the answers to these questions with your classmates.

1. In some countries, people can pay a company to freeze their bodies after they die. They hope that people in the future can bring them back to life. What do you think about this?

2. Why do you think the Egyptians stopped building pyramids?

3. Should mummies be in museums for people to look at? Does this show respect to the dead people and their culture? Explain.

SECOND READING

A. READING

CULTURE SHOCK

I moved to another country when I was eighteen, and I have now lived there for ten years. By now, it is very comfortable for me to live in my new country. Although I was happy at first, after a while I began to feel miserable. Luckily for me, a friend of mine showed me how the process of adjusting to a new culture goes through distinct stages. Her explanations made me feel more secure because then I could predict how I would feel about my new home. According to my friend's explanation, there are four stages of cultural adjustment.

Initially, you feel happy in the new environment. It's new and it's exciting. You think that everything here is better than where you were before. My friend called this the "honeymoon" stage. The second stage comes very quickly, and it's almost unavoidable. Your initial love affair with your new country quickly turns to hate. Suddenly, you start to see everything that seems wrong with this country. It could be the traffic, the way people smile or don't smile, the customs about paying attention to time, or even the food. My friend told me that this unhappy feeling was quite natural and that I ought to notice it, but that I shouldn't pay too much attention to it. If I could just hold on and survive this culture shock period, she said I would arrive at the next stage: acceptance. This is the stage in which you realize that your new country is truly different from the one in which you grew up, but that there are no rights and wrongs in culture. It just is. Once you accept that, you can keep working toward your goals. However, she also said that there was a fourth stage, which she called the "at home" stage. At this stage, you feel at home in the new country, and you feel completely comfortable with your daily life. You know how to do small things like buy a newspaper, fill your car with gas, or book an airplane flight over the telephone.

What About You?
Have you ever experienced any of the stages of cultural adjustment? Discuss your experiences with a classmate.

To sum up, the four stages of cultural adjustment made a lot of sense to me, and I have passed through every one. However, what my friend didn't tell me is that when you return to your native country, you are very likely to go through the stages all over again! I have heard this called "re-entry shock." Knowing this helps me a lot as I travel back and forth between my native country and my adopted country.

B. PRACTICE ANALYZING THE MODEL ESSAY

With a classmate, discuss the answers to these questions about Model Essay.

1. Does the thesis statement have these things? (Check all that apply.)

   ☐ clear topic

   ☐ main idea

   ☐ predictor

2. How many steps are in the process?

3. Which organizational pattern is used in the essay?

READING SKILLS PRACTICE

PRACTICE 1

A. DISCUSS

1. Which of the greetings shown in the pictures do you use? Where do people use the others?

2. When you learn a new language, what do you need to know in addition to the words and grammar? How do you learn this?

"In addition to what we say with our verbal language, we are constantly communicating our real feelings in our silent language—the language of behavior."

Edward T. Hall, *The Silent Language*, 1959

B. ABOUT THE READING

"Smile" is from the personal story of Mark Grottel as told to Al Santoli for his book, *New Americans*. Mark Grottel is a Russian Jew who came to New York with his wife and daughter in 1979. Jews were finally permitted to leave the former Soviet Union in the 1970s, and many left to escape anti-Semitism, or hatred of Jews. Most of them went to Israel, Canada, Australia, and the United States. Mr. Grottel was a physics professor in Leningrad, but after he migrated, he worked in a nuclear-engineering firm in New York because he could not get a job as a professor.

C. BEFORE YOU READ

1. *Discuss these questions.*

1. What situations have you been in where you did not understand a local custom? Think of social, work, and school situations.

2. What problem or problems did you have, and how did you feel in the situation?

2. Previewing

Read the title and paragraph 1 of "Smile." Then answer the questions.

1. Who is telling the story?

2. Where does the story take place?

3. Do you think it will be amusing or serious? Why?

3. *Before you read, refer to First Reading, below. Your purpose for the first reading is to be able to answer those questions.*

D. READING

SMILE

by Mark Grottel as told to Al Santoli

firm
company

cried out
spoke loudly

1   I have to tell you my favorite story about America. It was maybe one month after I began working at my first job in New York, at an engineering **firm**. Every day I sat at my desk, concentrating very hard. I was very serious. The problem was that I couldn't speak English and I was trying to learn new skills. My co-workers would pass back and forth in front of my desk. But, I was concentrating so heavily that I didn't pay attention to them.

2   One day a group of people came to the office. They just stood there looking at me. I didn't pay attention to them. One of these guys **cried out** very loud, "SMILE."

3   At first I didn't realize that he was talking to me. I looked up and saw everybody looking at me. He repeated, "SMILE."

4   My supervisor said to him, "Sir, this man just came from Russia. He has a problem with English." The man said, "Okay. He cannot talk. But, still, he can smile."

5   I understood what they were saying. So I started to smile. And everybody started to smile. When the group of men left the office, I was told that the man was a vice-president of our company.

6   I always think about this incident and laugh. Because in Russia, if you smile during working hours, your boss will say, "You are not working. You are just wasting time." When a supervisor comes into the work area, suddenly everybody becomes very serious. Here it is just the opposite. The vice-president couldn't understand why I was so serious. He was trying to cheer me up.

7   For the first time, I understood that in this country everybody has to smile.

E. FIRST READING

Answer these questions.

1. Why didn't Mark pay attention to the people in his office?

2. Who visited the office on that day?

3. How did the visitor respond?

F. Second Reading

1. Categorizing Information

Learning to organize information is a good study skill because it helps you understand and remember the ideas. If you can separate what happens in Russia from what happens in the United States, you will see the differences more clearly and be ready to discuss the material and review for a test.

Read the statements. Then read the selection again. Write R *on the line if the statement applies to Russia as Mark Grottel described it, and write* US *if it applies to the United States.*

1. ____ You can be friendly and smile and do a lot of work at the same time.

2. ____ Employees are supposed to be serious while they are working.

3. ____ If employees are not serious, supervisors think they are not working.

4. ____ Everybody is supposed to be friendly in the workplace.

G. Vocabulary Building

Read the underlined word or expression in its context and match it with the correct meaning. The paragraph number is in parentheses. Use a dictionary if necessary.

1. ____ Every day I sat at my desk, <u>concentrating</u> very hard. (¶1)

2. ____ . . . I was trying to learn new <u>skills</u>. (¶1)

3. ____ My <u>co-workers</u> would pass back and forth in front of my desk. (¶1)

4. ____ My co-workers would pass <u>back and forth</u> in front of my desk. (¶1)

5. ____ . . . I didn't <u>realize</u> that he was talking to me. (¶3)

6. ____ I always think about this <u>incident</u> and laugh. (¶6)

7. ____ . . . your <u>boss</u> will say, "You are not working." (¶6)

8. ____ "You are just <u>wasting time</u>." (¶6)

9. ____ He was trying to <u>cheer me up</u>. (¶6)

a. supervisor, superior in a workplace

b. not using your time well

c. event, occurrence, something that happens

d. abilities

e. make me happy

f. thinking very carefully

g. understand, know

h. people who work with you

i. in one direction and then in the opposite direction

PRACTICE 2

A. BEFORE YOU READ

Check (✓) the boxes that are true for your culture. Then compare answers as a class.

	Usually	**Sometimes**	**Rarely**
1. People kiss to say hello when they meet each other.			
2. Parents kiss their children.			
3. Couples kiss in public places.			
4. People kiss to say good-bye when they leave each other.			

Learn the meanings of the following words and phrases before you read the article. The numbers in parentheses indicate the paragraph where the word first appears in the article.

vary (2)	deal (4)	associated with (3)
represent (4)	make up (3)	instead of (5)
documents (4)		

B. READING

KISSING YOUR WAY AROUND THE WORLD

1   What are the customs for kissing people in your country? Do you kiss your relatives when you visit them? Do you kiss your friends hello when you meet them? Is it polite to kiss someone in public places in your country? All of these kissing customs depend on where in the world you are. Kissing may seem as universal as language, but in fact, kissing customs differ around the world.

2   In many places, kisses are used for saying hello. If you are in Europe or South America, you will see lots of these greeting kisses. But the kissing customs for greeting people vary from country to country, and traveling to new places can be confusing if you don't know them. Many European men and women say hello with two kisses, one on each cheek. But three kisses are polite in Belgium, and young people in Paris often prefer four. In these countries, you *must* start with the right cheek. Starting with your left cheek would be as awkward as sticking out your left hand for a handshake. A variation on the cheek kiss is found in Brazil. When women meet, they put their cheeks together and kiss the air. In some cultures, men kiss each other on the cheeks at business meetings. It's like shaking hands. In some parts of the world, people don't kiss when they meet each other. In fact, kissing in public is considered impolite. In Japan and China, for example, people in public places rarely kiss each other. In most Middle Eastern countries, men and women do not kiss in public, either.

3   Kisses aren't just for saying hello; people kiss for lots of other reasons as well. For example, a kiss can also be a sign of respect. Some people show respect by kissing religious articles and flags. Others kiss the ground when they come home to a country they love. Europeans and Latin Americans also use kisses to say "beautiful!" They kiss their fingertips when they see a pretty woman, an expensive car, or a great soccer play. In other places, people say good-bye by kissing their fingertips and blowing the kiss away. Kisses are associated with good luck, too. The French started the custom of kissing their cards for good luck before playing, and today, some people kiss a pair of dice before they roll them. The English kissed hurt fingers to make them better, as many mothers still do today. And, of course, people also kiss to make up after a fight.

Kissing Through History

4   Kissing was even more common in the past. In ancient Rome and Greece, for example, people kissed a lot. They kissed family, friends, and even strangers. The Romans sometimes kissed anyone they met on the hand, the cheek, or the mouth. They often put a perfume such as myrrh in their mouths to make the kisses more pleasant. They also kissed the hands, feet, and robes of kings and queens. Students kissed their teachers' hands. During the Middle Ages[1], kisses were used to make a promise. Kings and knights[2] kissed each other in special ceremonies. The knight's kiss was a promise to fight for the king. In return, the king's kiss was a promise to give the knight land and money. In the past, people kissed documents to show that they promised to keep the agreement. Back then, many people couldn't write their names, so they signed papers with an X. The X was their signature. Then they kissed the X to show that they promised to keep the deal. People still use Xs today, but they have nothing to do with promises. Some people like to sign cards and letters with Xs at the bottom. The Xs represent kisses. When you put Xs in your letter, it means you are sending kisses to the person to whom you are writing.

5   In other places, kissing was not very common at all. In some cultures, for instance, people rubbed their noses together instead of kissing. In Malaysia and Polynesia, people would just put their noses close to each other's faces and sniff. The ancient Egyptians probably did this, too. In fact, in several languages, the word for "kiss" means "smell."

6   Kissing will probably still be around a thousand years from now, but the rules may keep changing. Remember that kissing customs depend on where you are and that in some parts of the world kissing in public places is considered impolite.

[1]**Middle Ages**—the period in European history between the fifth and fifteenth centuries A.D.
[2]**knight**—in the Middle Ages, a man with a high rank who fought while riding a horse

C. After You Read

1. *Read these statements. If a statement is true according to the article, write* T *on the line. If it is false, write* F.

1. _F_ A kiss means the same thing all over the world.

2. ____ In many places, a kiss is a kind of greeting.

3. ____ In some countries, it is not polite for people to kiss in public.

4. ____ In the past, kisses were used to make a promise.

5. ___ The ancient Romans rarely kissed each other.

6. ___ Kisses can be a sign of respect.

2. Identifying the Main Idea of a Paragraph

Most paragraphs have one main idea. Good readers try to find the **main idea of a paragraph** as they read. Identifying the main idea of a paragraph will help you understand the meaning. Sometimes one sentence of a paragraph (often the first or last) expresses the main idea. Other times, you need to use all of the information in the paragraph to figure out the main idea.

Check (✓) the statement that expresses the main idea in each group.

1.

☐ a. Young Parisians kiss four times when they meet.

☑ b. Kissing customs for greeting people differ from country to country.

☐ c. Many Europeans say hello with two kisses, one on each cheek.

2.

☐ a. Kisses are also associated with good luck.

☐ b. For example, a kiss can also be a sign of respect.

☐ c. Kisses aren't just for saying hello; people kiss for lots of other reasons as well.

3.

☐ a. Kissing was even more common in the past.

☐ b. In ancient Rome and Greece, for example, people kissed a lot.

☐ c. During the Middle Ages in Europe, kisses were used to make a promise.

4.

☐ a. In some cultures, for instance, people rubbed their noses together instead of kissing.

☐ b. In other places, kissing was not very common at all.

☐ c. In Malaysia and Polynesia, people would just put their noses close to each other's faces and sniff.

D. Vocabulary

1. *Match each word or phrase with the correct definition.*

Word or Phrase	Definition
1. _c_ vary	a. connected in your mind with something else
2. ___ deal	b. to symbolize or stand for
3. ___ documents	c. to differ
4. ___ represent	d. to become friends with someone again after an argument
5. ___ make up	

6. ____ associated with   e. an agreement

7. ____ instead of   f. in place of someone or something

                g. official papers

2. *Complete each sentence with the correct word or phrase from Exercise 1.*

1. I heard you had an argument with Eva. Did you ____ *make up* ____ yet?

2. Please sign all of these _____.

3. Some people bow or shake hands _____ kissing.

4. I promise to keep the _____ we are making.

5. The meanings of kisses _____ from one culture to another.

6. In some places, a kiss is _____ good luck.

7. The Xs at the bottom of a letter _____ kisses.

E. Learning Synonyms

Synonyms are words that have similar meanings. For example, *vary* and *differ* are synonyms because they mean almost the same thing. Learning synonyms can help you improve your vocabulary.

Read the paragraph. Find a synonym for each word or phrase in the chart that follows. Write the synonyms in the chart.

    Humans are not the only animals that kiss. For instance, chimpanzees sometimes greet each other with little pecks on the cheek. Other times, they give wide-mouthed kisses when they greet another chimp. They also kiss to make up after a fight. When prairie dogs meet, they kiss each other to discover who is a family member and who is a stranger. Fish called "kissing gouramis" press their mouths together like suction cups.

Word	Synonym
1. kisses	*pecks*
2. argument	
3. find out	
4. people	
5. for example	
6. outsider	
7. become friends again	

F. Discussion

From the article, you learned that customs related to kissing vary from culture to culture. The same is true for many other customs. Discuss these questions as a class.

1. *Using names:* When do you call people by their first names? When can you use nicknames?

2. *Tipping:* Is tipping common in your country? Who do you usually tip? How much do you tip?

3. *Being on time:* Is it important to be on time in your culture? Are there some times when it's OK to be late?

4. *Taking off your shoes:* Do you take off your shoes when you enter a home? Is it impolite to keep your shoes on?

5. *Giving gifts:* When do you give gifts? Are there any cultural rules for gift giving? Are some gifts considered inappropriate?

Above material from: *For Your Information 3, Second Edition*

PRACTICE 3

A. BEFORE YOU READ

Talk with a partner.

1. You're going to read a love story. It's about two people from opposite sides of the world. What are some possible challenges for them?

2. How important is it for married people to have things in common[1] with each other? Choose a number between 1 (extremely important) and 4 (not important at all). Explain your answer.

[1]have things in common = share the same interests, experiences, beliefs, etc.

B. READING

Look at the words and definitions next to the reading. Then read without stopping.

"IT WAS LOVE"

[1]an *exchange student* = someone who studies for a while at a foreign university

1   Arunaa was in her last year of college near her home in Malaysia. It was the first day of a new course, and she was in class. "Suddenly," she says, "I had this **awful** feeling of being watched." She looked across the room. Someone was **staring** at her—an exchange student[1] from Europe. He **went on** looking at her all through the class. He did it the next day, too, and the next. Finally, she told herself, "Enough! I'm going to talk to him. That will stop him." So she went and sat down next to him.

She **discovered** that his name was Hervé, and he was French. "As soon as we started talking, it was magic and he was perfect."

2   Arunaa and Hervé fell in love. But after a few months, he had to return to France. Soon afterwards, Arunaa graduated and **faced** the biggest decision of her life. Hervé wanted her to join him in Paris. Should she go, or should she try to forget him?

3   Arunaa remembers, "My parents were in **total** shock. But the best thing was that they never said no. It was always my choice and my **responsibility**. This is what they always taught me, to make my own decisions."

4   It was hard for Arunaa to think of leaving family, friends, and home. Living in France would be a challenge, too. For one thing, she did not speak French. "And it was difficult for me," she says, "because I wasn't really sure what to expect. When I met Hervé, he was a student, and almost like a tourist.[2] He was happy in Malaysia and he felt **comfortable** there, but that wasn't real life for him. I was about to meet another Hervé, whom I didn't know—the Hervé who was **no longer** a student, but a man with a serious job, and a Frenchman in his own country."

5   Arunaa decided to go. "I had to take the chance.[3] **Although** there were many **differences** between us, we were so much **alike**! I knew that he was the one for me." For Arunaa and Hervé, it was the right decision. Now, they are happily married.

6   **Marriage** is not easy. It is even harder when a **couple** has to deal with differences in language, religion, and culture. Arunaa says, "The cultural differences were enormous.[4] I come from an Islamic country, although my family is Christian, and many things in France shocked me." The hardest thing, she says, is to understand the way that French people think.

7   Smaller differences in their everyday life caused problems, too. Arunaa laughs, "We are like night and day![5] I eat rice three times a day, and I don't wear shoes in the house. Also, I want to take care of my husband, like my mother and her mother before her, but that makes Hervé uncomfortable." Even with all the **difficulties**, after seven years, they are still very much in love.

[2] *a tourist* = someone who is traveling for fun

[3] *take the chance* = do something that may be dangerous

[4] *enormous* = very, very big

[5] *like night and day* = complete opposites

C. COMPREHENSION CHECK

Read these sentences. Circle T (true) or F (false).

1. Arunaa is a young woman from Malaysia.   T   F

2. She met Hervé when she was a college student in France.   T   F

3. Arunaa's parents told her not to leave home.   T   F

4. Arunaa and Hervé are now married and living in France.   T   F

5. It was hard for Arunaa to get used to many things in her new life. T   F

D. VOCABULARY

1. *Find the four verbs in **bold** in "'It Was Love.'" Add them to the chart. Use the base form of each verb.*

	Nouns	Verbs	Adjectives	Other
1			awful	
2				
3			total	
	responsibility			
4			comfortable	
				no longer
5				although
	difference			
			alike	
6	marriage			
	couple			
7	difficulty			

2. *Which words are new to you? Circle them in the chart. Then find the words in the reading. Look at the context. Can you guess the meaning?*

3. *These sentences are **about the reading**. What is the meaning of each **boldfaced** word or phrase? Circle a, b, or c.*

1. Arunaa saw someone new across the room. He was **staring** at her. *Stare* means

   a. speak, talk.   b. point a finger.   c. keep looking.

2. The exchange student **went on** looking at Arunaa, day after day. *Go on* means

   a. stop.   b. continue.   c. disappear.

3. She talked to him and **discovered** that he was French. *Discover* means

   a. find out, learn.   b. tell, say.   c. consider.

4. Arunaa had to **face** a big decision. *Face* means

   a. turn into.   b. deal with.   c. turn out.

5. Hervé felt **comfortable** in Malaysia. It was good to be there. If you are comfortable, you are

   a. stressed.   b. bored.   c. feeling good.

6. **Although** there were many differences between Arunaa and Hervé, they were the same in important ways. Use *although* to introduce the first part of a sentence when the second part

   a. gives a reason.   b. repeats the first part.   c. may seem surprising.

7. Arunaa says they are different in some ways but **alike** in others. *Alike* means

   a. the same or nearly the same.   b. disappointed, unhappy.   c. the opposite.

8. Arunaa and Hervé are married. They have a good **marriage**. *Marriage* means

   a. a plan for the future.   b. the relationship between a husband and wife.   c. a memory of the past.

9. This is the story of a **couple** from two different cultures. *A couple* means

   a. a change in ideas and traditions.   b. two people in a relationship.   c. a problem or trouble.

10. It's not easy to be married. There are even more **difficulties** in cross-cultural marriages. *Difficulty* means something that is

   a. fun.   b. hard.   c. new.

4. *These sentences use the target words and phrases **in new contexts**. Complete them with the words and phrases in the box.*

alike	comfortable	difficulties	face	marriage
although	couple	discovered	go on	stare

1. We looked out the window and _____ that it was snowing.

2. In my country, it's not polite to _____ at people. What about in yours?

3. _____ he's not tall, he's a good basketball player.

4. Finally, the judge said to the _____, "You are now husband and wife."

5. Good communication between husband and wife is important for a strong _____.

6. You can't run away from this problem. You have to _____ it.

7. Suddenly, the TV screen went black and a voice said, "We are experiencing technical _____."

8. I was _____ in bed, and I didn't want to get up.

9. She and her sister look _____, but they dress very differently.

10. We can't afford to _____ spending money like this. We have to stop.

5. *Read each definition and look at the paragraph number. Look back at the reading to find the* **boldfaced** *word or phrase to match the definition. Copy it in the chart.*

Definition	Paragraph	Target Word or Phrase
1. very bad, terrible	1	
2. complete	3	
3. something you have to do or take care of	3	
4. not now, not anymore	4	
5. ways that two people or things are not like each other	5	

E. WORD GRAMMAR

1. *Complete each sentence with a phrasal verb. Use* come out, deal with, figure out, go on, pick up, turn into, *or* turn out. *There is one extra verb.*

1. Work, classes, taking care of your children—that's a lot for you to _____!

2. Luis is driving to the airport to _____ his parents.

3. I'm sure everything will _____ well in the end.

4. Their discussions sometimes _____ fights.

5. We need help. We can't _____ what to do.

6. I'm sure he won't quit. He'll _____ trying.

2. *On a piece of paper, write three sentences with phrasal verbs from Part 1.*

F. IDENTIFYING PARAGRAPH TOPICS

What is each paragraph in the reading about? Write the topics of the paragraphs.

1. Paragraph 1: _____ *how Arunaa and Harvé met* _____

2. Paragraph 2: _____

3. Paragraph 3: _____

4. Paragraph 4: _____

5. Paragraph 5: _____

6. Paragraph 6: _____

7. Paragraph 7: _____

G. READING FOR DETAILS

Are these statements about the reading true or false? If the reading doesn't give the information, check (✓) "It doesn't say."

	True	False	It doesn't say
1. Arunaa met Hervé in a college classroom in Malaysia.	☐	☐	☐
2. Hervé left before Arunaa graduated.	☐	☐	☐
3. Arunaa expected him to come back.	☐	☐	☐
4. Arunaa's parents told her not to go to France.	☐	☐	☐
5. Hervé expected things to be easy for her in France.	☐	☐	☐
6. Arunaa says her biggest challenge was religious differences.	☐	☐	☐
7. In France, Arunaa still eats rice three times a day.	☐	☐	☐
8. Arunaa can speak French well now.	☐	☐	☐

H. READING BETWEEN THE LINES

"Reading between the lines" means understanding meaning that is hidden or is not given openly. Readers have to make **inferences**—guesses that they base on the information given and what they already know.

Answer these questions with your own opinions.

1. Why was Hervé staring at Arunaa in class? _____

   _____

2. Why were Arunaa's parents in shock? _____

   _____

3. What worried Arunaa most when she thought about going to France? _____

   _____

4. Why doesn't Arunaa wear shoes in the house? _____

   _____

5. Why is Hervé uncomfortable with the way that Arunaa wants to take care of him?

   _____

   _____

I. SHARING OPINIONS

Talk about the following opinions in a small group. Tell why you agree or disagree.

Opinion 1: Your parents' opinion of the person you marry is very important.

Opinion 2: People should decide for themselves about marriage. They—and not their families—should have total responsibility for the decision.

Opinion 3: It's better to marry someone who is as much like you as possible.

Unit Four

Do You Believe It?

READING 1

Read the list of actions that different cultures believe bring good luck or bad luck. Check (✓) whether you think the action brings good luck, brings bad luck, or has no effect. Then compare answers in a small group.

Action	Brings Good Luck	Brings Bad Luck	Has No Effect
1. breaking a mirror			
2. carrying a rabbit's foot			
3. seeing a black cat			
4. opening an umbrella indoors			

Action	Brings Good Luck	Brings Bad Luck	Has No Effect
5. crossing your fingers			
6. finding a four-leaf clover			
7. walking under a ladder			
8. knocking on wood			
9. seeing a moving star			
10. spilling salt			
11. washing your hair on the day of a test			
12. finding money on the street			

A. BEFORE YOU READ

1. *Discuss these questions with a partner.*

1. What numbers are considered good luck in your country?

2. What numbers are considered bad luck in your country?

2. *You are going to read about lucky and unlucky numbers. Check (✓) the statements about this topic that you think are true. Then compare answers with a partner.*

☐ 1. Different cultures have different ideas about which numbers are lucky and which are unlucky.

☐ 2. Lucky and unlucky numbers are based on science.

☐ 3. Superstitions about numbers are an important part of everyone's everyday life.

☐ 4. People in ancient times thought some numbers brought good luck and others brought bad luck.

☐ 5. All people agree that the number 13 brings bad luck.

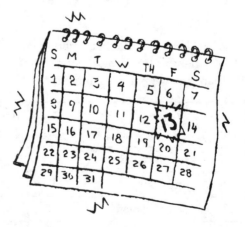

3. *Learn the meanings of the following words before you read the article.*

notion (1)	rearranging (5)
skip (2)	acquire (7)
feast (3)	security (9)
banned (4)	

B. READING

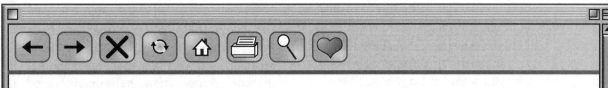

IT'S YOUR LUCKY NUMBER!

1   Do you think some numbers are lucky and others are unlucky? Most cultures have good luck and bad luck numbers. The notion that numbers can bring good luck or bad luck is a superstition.

Unlucky Numbers

2   The number 13 is considered unlucky by superstitious people in North and South America and in Europe. It is such a strong superstition that many airlines do not have a Flight 13. Lots of planes don't have a Row 13, either. The same is true for tall buildings. If you are in an elevator, you may notice that there is no button for the 13th floor. The buttons go from 12 to 14 and skip 13. Some people avoid starting trips or other activities on the 13th day of a month. The English language even has a word for the fear of the number 13. It's *triskaidekaphobia*. Are you triskaidekaphobic?

3   We do not know how the number 13 came to be considered unlucky. There are several theories. One is that it comes from the ancient Roman belief that 13 was a sign of death and destruction. Other people think it all started with an old Viking[1] story about a feast for twelve gods. The evil god, Loki, was not invited, but he came anyway. That made thirteen guests. According to the story, Loki killed one of the other gods. Since then, the number 13 has been considered bad luck. Some superstitious people believe it is unlucky for thirteen to eat dinner together. One of them will die within a year. Another story comes from Christianity. There were thirteen people at the last supper of Jesus Christ. The next day, he was killed.

4   While 13 is considered unlucky in the West, in many Asian countries, such as China, Japan, and Korea, the number 4 is an unlucky number. That's because the word for *four* sounds like the word for *death*. In Asia, many hotels have no 4th floor. In Seoul's Inchon Airport, there are no gates 4 or 44. And you won't find the 4th or 14th floors in many Chinese buildings. Chinese people often avoid using 4 in their phone numbers, home addresses, and license plates. Two Chinese cities even banned the numeral 4 from license plates. In all of these countries, it's a bad idea to give gifts in sets of four.

5   The numbers 13 and 4 are not the only ones associated with bad luck. For example, 17 is considered unlucky in Italy because rearranging the letters in the Roman numerals for 17 could spell VIXI which means "I lived" (or "I'm dead") in Latin. The number 9 can also bring bad luck in some places. *Nine* is pronounced as "ku" in Japanese, which is similar to the word *pain*. Hospitals usually don't have 9th floors in Japan.

[1]**Viking**—refers to the Scandinavians who invaded Europe from the eighth to the eleventh centuries

Lucky Numbers

6   Just as some numbers are supposed to be bad luck, there are some numbers that are considered lucky. For example, 7 is considered a lucky number by some superstitious people in Western cultures. Why is 7 lucky? No one knows for sure where the idea came from, but there are many special 7s: seven days of the week, seven Wonders of the World, seven colors of the spectrum, and so on.

7   In China, many people believe that 8 is a very lucky number. Why? The word for *eight* sounds like the word for *to acquire wealth* or *to become rich*. People pay extra fees to get 8s in their phone numbers, home addresses, and license plate numbers. In Hong Kong, it can cost millions of dollars to get a numeral 8 on your license plate. The number 8 is so lucky that the mayor of Beijing announced that the 2008 Olympic Games in Beijing would begin at 8:00 p.m. on August 8!

8   Three is also a lucky number in China because the word for *three* sounds like the word for *life*. A man in Beijing paid $215,000 to get the luckiest cell phone number: 133-3333-3333.

9   In fact, there is nothing lucky or unlucky about any number. Still, many people believe that a number can bring good or bad luck. Most of us have fears that make us feel insecure. Superstitions help us overcome these fears by providing security. With all the uncertainty in the world, one thing is certain: None of us knows what tomorrow will bring.

C. AFTER YOU READ

1. Making Inferences

Write the number of the paragraph that answers each question.

1. Why do some people believe that the number 8 is lucky? _____

2. Where is the number 4 considered unlucky? _____

3. What theories are there about how the number 13 came to be considered unlucky? _____

4. What are some examples of superstitions associated with the number 13? _____

5. What numbers, besides 13 and 4, are considered unlucky in some cultures? _____

2. *Check (✓) the statements that are inferences based on information in the article.*

☐ 1. Numbers were important in some ancient societies.

☐ 2. There are only three theories about how the number 13 came to be considered unlucky.

☐ 3. Starting a new job on the 13th day of the month could be a problem for some people who are superstitious.

☐ 4. Superstitions are based on scientific facts.

☐ 5. Some superstitious people would not invite thirteen people to a dinner party.

☐ 6. Many Chinese would be happy to have the number 8 in their phone number.

☐ 7. There is scientific proof that the number 7 has special powers.

D. VOCABULARY

1. *Complete each sentence with the correct word(s).*

acquired	rearrange	banned	security
feast	skip	notion	

1. I'll _____ my schedule so I can have lunch with you on Friday at noon. But that means I'll have to _____ a meeting at work.

2. Guns, knives, cigarette lighters, and scissors are just a few of the things that are _____ on planes. This should provide more _____ to passengers.

3. After years of hard work as a collector, Mr. Lee _____ both wealth and many valuable stamps.

4. In many stories, a great _____ is given to honor the birth of a prince.

5. The _____ that 13 is an unlucky number is probably thousands of years old.

2. *Circle the letter of the correct answer.*

1. If you <u>skipped</u> your friend's graduation party, you _____.

   a. went to it   b. did not go to it

2. If you have job <u>security</u>, you _____.

   a. are afraid of losing your job   b. aren't worried about losing your job

3. When a museum <u>acquires</u> some new paintings, it _____.

   a. gives them away   b. gets them from somewhere

4. At a <u>feast</u>, you would have _____.

   a. interesting books and movies   b. lots of good food

5. If you accept the <u>notion</u> that some numbers bring bad luck, you _____.

   a. believe it   b. don't believe it

6. If smoking is <u>banned</u> in an airport, you _____.

   a. can smoke there   b. cannot smoke there

7. If you <u>rearrange</u> the furniture in your living room, the room _____.

   a. looks different   b. looks the same

3. *Cross out the word or phrase in each group that does not belong.*

1. idea	notion	belief	fact
2. skip	omit	add	leave out
3. prohibit	ban	allow	forbid
4. meal	feast	banquet	exercise
5. security	concern	safety	protection
6. gain	acquire	lose	get

4. Learning Homonyms

Read these sentences. Write the meaning and part of speech of each underlined word. You may need to use your dictionary.

1. a. There is no <u>row</u> 13 on this plane.
    Meaning: _____
    Part of speech: _____
    b. My arms are tired from <u>rowing</u> the boat.
    Meaning: _____
    Part of speech: _____

2. a. The floor numbers <u>skip</u> 13. They go from 12 to 14.
    Meaning: _____
    Part of speech: _____
    b. My daughter learned to <u>skip</u> when she was three.
    Meaning: _____
    Part of speech: _____

3. a. Please push the <u>button</u> for the 12th floor.
    Meaning: _____
    Part of speech: _____
    b. You need to <u>button</u> your coat; it's windy outside.
    Meaning: _____
    Part of speech: _____

4. a. The little boy <u>tripped</u> when he walked into the room.
    Meaning: _____
    Part of speech: _____
    b. How was your <u>trip</u> to New York?
    Meaning: _____
    Part of speech: _____

5. a. There's a <u>sign</u> for a gas station. We'd better stop here.
    Meaning: _____
    Part of speech: _____
    b. Did you <u>sign</u> the lease for your new apartment yet?
    Meaning: _____
    Part of speech: _____

USING GRAPHIC ORGANIZERS: MAKING A CHART

Read the paragraph and complete the chart that follows with information from the paragraph.

FOOD AND SUPERSTITIONS

Many societies around the world have superstitions connected with food. The ancient Egyptians, for example, thought onions kept evil spirits away. When they took an oath (made a promise), they placed one hand on an onion. The custom of throwing rice at weddings goes back to the time in Europe when people thought rice, a symbol of health and prosperity, would calm evil spirits so they would not bother the wedding couple. In Hungary, superstitious people throw salt on the door of a new house to protect them from evil spirits. Superstitious Europeans used to put mustard seeds on the roof of their homes to keep vampires away. In Japan, during the festival of Setsuben, people put beans in dark corners and entrances of the home to drive out evil spirits. For many years, Europeans have used garlic as a charm against evil spirits. Some wore garlic around their necks. Others placed garlic over their doors for protection.

Food	Superstition	Place of Origin	Effect
1. onion	placing a hand on an onion while taking an oath	Egypt	kept evil spirits away
2.			
3.			
4.			
5.			
6.			

Discuss these questions as a class.

1. Do you have a lucky number? If so, what is it? How did you choose it? When do you use your lucky number?

2. What are some food superstitions in your country? Do you know where they came from?

READING 2

A. BEFORE YOU READ

1. *Discuss these questions with a partner.*

1. What superstitions do you know that relate to sports?

2. Are there any famous athletes in your country who are known for their superstitions?

3. Why do you think so many athletes are superstitious?

2. Skimming for the Main Idea

Skim the article one time. Then choose the statement you think describes the main idea.

1. Many athletes are superstitious.

2. Some athletes dress the same way every day.

3. Some sports superstitions are strange.

3. *Learn the meanings of the following words and phrases before you read the article.*

passed up (2)	illusion (3)	quirk (5)	weird (8)
rituals (3)	stick to (3)	hung up on (5)	

B. Reading

Superstitious Athletes

by Walter Roessing

1   Did you know that golfer Tiger Woods always wears a red shirt on the last day of a tournament? Or that basketball superstar Michael Jordan always wore his blue University of North Carolina shorts under his Chicago Bulls uniform? Racecar driver Mario Andretti wouldn't enter a car from the right side. Are you surprised that hockey star and coach Wayne Gretzsky won't get his hair cut when his team plays away games because they lost one night after he got a haircut? All of these athletes have one thing in common: They are all superstitious.

2   "Athletes are more superstitious than most people," says Oakland Raiders football player Ronnie Lott. He always wears his lucky swim shorts under his uniform. The one time he forgot to wear his lucky shorts for a game, he hurt his shoulder. "Athletes do all kinds of crazy things to guarantee victory or make sure they won't get hurt." Lott has food superstitions, too. He always eats a hamburger the night before a game. Several years ago, his team was playing an away game on Thanksgiving Day. The night before, Lott passed up a turkey dinner with his teammates to dine alone at Wendy's.

3   Thomas Tutko is a sports psychologist. He says, "Whatever the superstitions, they help athletes and coaches relax." They give players the illusion of control. Superstitious beliefs often involve rituals about uniforms, food, or numbers. Many athletes think if they stick to a routine, it will help them win. Tutko recalls working with San Jose-area high school basketball players who believed they were winning because of their white socks. "They refused to wash their socks all season," Tutko says.

4   Athletes have been known to wear the same uniforms without washing them until their team loses. Other athletes always get dressed in a specific sequence. They say these rituals bring them good luck. The famous boxer Joe Louis believed that he would lose a fight if his right glove was put on before the left one. Baseball pitcher Turk Wendell brushed his teeth and ate licorice candy between every inning[1]. Los Angeles Dodgers player Nomar Garciaparra gets dressed the same way every day. He also makes sure to step on each step of the dugout with both feet, and he taps his toes when it is his turn to bat.

5   Former baseball player Wade Boggs is almost as famous for his superstitions as he is for his athletic ability. He ate chicken before every game. That quirk started when Boggs was playing in the minor leagues[2]. "On the days when I ate chicken, I always got two hits," he says. Boggs was hung up on the numbers 7 and 17, too. Before a night game, he always ran in the outfield at exactly 7:17 P.M.

6   Boggs isn't the only athlete with superstitions about numbers. Mario Andretti wouldn't stay in a hotel room with the numeral 13. Baltimore Orioles pitcher Jose Mercedes had a problem with the number 3. He wouldn't pitch in the third game of a season.

7   Tony La Russa was the manager of the St. Louis Cardinals baseball team. He has an unusual superstition involving writing: He prints the names of the players'

[1]**inning** one of the nine playing periods in the game of baseball
[2]**minor leagues** the groups of teams that form the lower levels of American professional baseball

batting order for every game until they lose. Then he switches to cursive writing. When St. Louis loses again, he goes back to printing.

8   Some rituals seem very weird. Here's an example: Mark van Eeghen played football for the Oakland Raiders. Before each game, he climbed on top of the television set in his hotel room and jumped to the bed. He felt that this would protect him from getting hurt on the field. But one time, he missed the bed and fell. His injury forced him to miss a game.

9   It seems some athletes will do anything for good luck!

C. AFTER YOU READ

1. *Write the answer to each question. Then, compare answers with a partner.*

1. Why do some athletes believe in superstitions?

_____

2. According to sports psychologist Thomas Tutko, what is the benefit of superstitions?

_____

3. What three areas do superstitious beliefs often involve?

_____

2. Using Graphic Organizers: Making a Chart

Complete the chart with information from the article.

Name of Athlete	Sport	Superstitions
1 Tiger Woods	*golf*	*wears a red shirt on the last day of a tournament*
2.	basketball	
3. Mario Andretti		
4.		won't get his hair cut when his team plays away games
5. Ronnie Lott		
6.	boxing	
7. Turk Wendell		
8.		gets dressed the same way; steps on each step of the dugout with both feet, and taps his toes when it's his turn to bat
9.	baseball	
10.		wouldn't pitch in the third game of a season
11. Tony La Russa		
12.	football	

3. Identifying Facts and Opinions

Decide if each statement is a fact or an opinion. Check (✓) the correct box.

	Fact	Opinion
1. Mario Andretti wouldn't enter a car from the right side.		
2. Athletes do all kinds of crazy things to guarantee victory or make sure they won't get hurt.		
3. Thomas Tutko is a sports psychologist.		
4. Former baseball player Wade Boggs is almost as famous for his superstitions as he is for his athletic ability.		
5. Before a night game, Boggs always ran in the outfield at exactly 7:17 p.m.		
6. Some rituals seem very weird.		
7. Mark van Eeghen played football for the Oakland Raiders.		
8. It seems some athletes will do anything for good luck!		

D. VOCABULARY

1. *Match each word or phrase with the correct definition.*

Word or Phrase	Definition
1. _____ pass up	a. strange
2. _____ illusion	b. to follow
3. _____ quirk	c. something that is not what it seems to be
4. _____ stick to	d. a set of actions always done in the same way
5. _____ ritual	e. worried about something
6. _____ hung up on	f. an unusual habit
7. _____ weird	g. to decide not to take advantage of an opportunity

2. *Complete each sentence with the correct word or phrase from Exercise 1.*

1. Athletes like superstitions because they give them the _____ of control.

2. Most of us have a _____ or two that may seem odd.

3. Why did you _____ the chance to go to the concert?

4. What is that strange noise coming from the hall? It sounds really _____.

5. Don is _____ getting the highest grades in the class.

6. My daughter has a nightly _____. She always takes a bath, has a glass of milk, and reads a chapter in a book.

7. Please _____ the schedule I wrote on the blackboard.

READING 3

A. BEFORE YOU READ

1. Activate Your Background Knowledge: *To make good inferences, look for clues the author gives and relate them to what you know from other experiences in your own life.*

Discuss these questions with a partner.

1. Have you ever had your fortune told? What method did the fortune-teller use?

2. What did you learn from the fortune-teller? Was he or she right?

3. Do you think fortune-telling is simply a form of entertainment or do you think it is something more?

4. Is fortune-telling popular in your native culture? Which methods are the most popular?

2. Preview and Predict

Read the title and headings of the article on pages 108–110. Look at the pictures and read the captions. Can you guess what the article will be about? Think of three topics that might be discussed in the article.

1. _____

2. _____

3. _____

3. Preview the Vocabulary

The words in the box are boldfaced in the article on pages 108–110. Complete the Vocabulary Chart with words from the box. If necessary, use your dictionary.

Words to Watch			
palm	horoscope	reveal	forecast
aspect	analyze	compatible	
subconscious	psychologist	superstition	

Vocabulary Chart	
Word	**Definition**
	to show something that was previously hidden
	one of the parts or features of a situation, idea, or problem
	a description of your character and things that will happen to you, based on the position of the stars and planets when you were born
	able to live or work successfully with someone else

Vocabulary Chart	
Word	**Definition**
	a belief not based on scientific knowledge but connected with old ideas about magic; a belief that some objects or actions are lucky and some are unlucky
	a person who is trained in the scientific study of the mind, and how it works, and how mental problems can be treated
	the inside surface of your hand between the base of your fingers and your wrist
	related to the part of your mind in which there are thoughts and feelings that you do not realize that you have
	to examine or think about something carefully in order to understand it
	to say what is likely to happen in the future, based on information you have now

4. Set a Purpose

You are going to read an article about fortune-telling. What do you want to find out about this topic? Write two questions you would like the article to answer.

1. _____

2. _____

B. READING

As you read the article, think about the underlined words and phrases. Use context clues to guess the meaning of each word, and write it on the line given. Remember to look at the words and sentences that surround the underlined words.

FORTUNE-TELLING

1   What will the future bring? Adventure, an unexpected marriage, or a long journey? Methods of predicting the future through fortune-telling have existed for centuries. Although many people <u>dismiss</u> these practices as **superstitions**, others accept them, and fortune-telling remains popular in many cultures. From analyzing the formation of clouds to opening fortune cookies at a Chinese restaurant, people do numerous things to make predictions about the future.

dismiss: _____

It's All in the Hands

2   Reading **palms** has long been a favorite method of
fortune-telling. The shape of fingers, the appearance of fin-
gernails, and in particular the lines of the palm are important features for interpretation. Some say that there are
three main lines in the hand, the life line, heart line, and
head line, revealing intellectual and emotional aspects of
the person. Look at your own palm. Do you see the three
<u>dominant</u> lines? Gypsies, or the Roma, are famous for their
skill at reading palms. They are also well known for their
ability to interpret the images they see when they look into a <u>crystal ball</u>, a magic
glass ball that shows the future.

Reading palms is a
popular way to tell
someone's future.

dominant: _____

crystal ball: _____

Coffee or Tea?

3   A method of fortune-telling using coffee is practiced
throughout the world, especially in the Middle East. After the
coffee is drunk, the fortune-teller turns the cup several times
and then looks at the <u>coffee grounds</u>, the tiny pieces of coffee
beans left in the cup. She analyzes the shapes of the coffee
grounds, which supposedly have various meanings. For example, a shape like a tree at the bottom of the cup could mean
that positive changes are coming. Similarly, a form that looks
like fruit might <u>signify</u> prosperity or good fortune. Other shapes
have more obvious meanings to fortune-tellers. A heart could
forecast love, and a ring suggests a marriage in the future. The
patterns of tea leaves in the bottom of a teacup are used in a
similar manner as a means of fortune-telling.

Can the pattern
of tea leaves in
the bottom of
your cup predict
your future?

coffee grounds: _____

signify: _____

Symbolic Images

4   Tarot cards are also used to predict the future and to **analyze** a person's character. Dating back to the fifteenth century in Italy and perhaps originating from
somewhere in Asia, the cards are marked with various symbols and characters. A
few cards are selected, and they supposedly **reveal aspects** of a person's personality, major influences in his or her life, and maybe the direction of future actions.
It takes knowledge and skill to analyze the <u>significance</u> of the cards. The I-Ching,
an ancient Chinese book with symbols, is somewhat similar to Tarot cards. It also
requires <u>expertise</u> to interpret the meaning of the symbols.

significance: _____

expertise: _____

The Planets and Stars

5   From the earliest times, many cultures have shown interest in <u>astrology</u>, the study of how the movement of stars and planets affects human events. Still popular today, astrology utilizes the **horoscope**, or twelve signs of the Zodiac, and a description of your character and things that will happen to you based on the position of the stars and planets at the time of your birth. Some people use the horoscope to determine whether they are likely to get along with others in a relationship or even in a marriage. According to followers of astrology, some signs of the Zodiac are especially **compatible** and are more likely to result in a <u>harmonious</u> relationship, while others are incompatible and are likely to end up in a relationship filled with conflict. Some people read their horoscope on a daily basis in newspapers or websites for advice about whether they will experience good or bad luck and for suggestions for action to take in the future. To paraphrase the words of William Shakespeare, the famous sixteenth-century English writer, however, it is not in the stars to hold our destiny, but in ourselves.

astrology: _____

harmonious: _____

What Do Dreams Reveal?

6   Just as stars are considered by some to influence human actions, dreams are <u>regarded as</u> indicators of the future. Colors, images, and events occurring in dreams supposedly have special significance; some believe they reflect **subconscious** fears, concerns, or desires. Others believe that dreams can predict future events. For example, in Chinese legends, a dream of a rainbow predicts eventual good fortune. A number of modern **psychologists** encourage patients to write down their dreams as a way of analyzing their concerns or issues. In psychology, dreams are not viewed as definite predictors of future events but rather as a means of self-discovery, a way of reflecting on the direction of one's life.

regarded as: _____

A Means of Exploration

7   How many people actually believe in fortune-telling? Some insist that they have encountered fortune-tellers who appear to have special <u>psychic</u> powers that enable them to "see" the future. Others reject any form of fortune-telling as false and ridiculous. Some religions forbid fortune-telling in any form. Quite a few people, though, seem to enjoy various types of fortune-telling as forms of entertainment. At any rate, it is likely that fortune-telling will continue to appeal to those curious about the future. If not taken too seriously, fortune-telling can be viewed as an attempt to evaluate choices and possibly as a path to self-discovery.

psychic: _____

C. AFTER YOU READ

1. Check Your Comprehension

True or false? Write T (True) or F (False) next to each of the following statements. If a statement is false, rewrite it to make it true.

1. _____ In the past, people did not practice fortune-telling.

2. _____ Tea leaves and coffee grounds are used in a similar way to tell the future.

3. _____ Fortune-telling is practiced all over the world.

4. _____ Tarot cards and the I-Ching both require expertise in interpreting the symbols.

5. _____ Fortune-telling practices are frequently dismissed as superstitions.

6. _____ Coffee grounds are used in the Middle East to predict the future.

7. _____ The twelve signs of the Zodiac refer to the position of the stars.

8. _____ There are only a few ways to predict the future.

9. _____ It is a known fact that dreams indicate future events.

10. _____ Reading palms is a relatively recent way of predicting the future.

2. Use Context Clues

Work with a partner and compare the definitions you each wrote for the underlined words in the article. Talk about the clues and strategy you used to come up with your definition. Then, look up the words in a dictionary. How close was your guess to the dictionary definition? Do you think your strategy was successful? Why or why not?

3. Make Inferences

Put a check next to the inferences that you can make after reading "Fortune-Telling."

1. _____ A woman who believes in astrology might read her horoscope to see if her personality is compatible with her boyfriend's.

2. _____ William Shakespeare probably did not believe in astrology.

3. _____ Some people read their horoscope or go to fortune-tellers just for fun.

4. _____ The author believes that the shapes of coffee grounds are true predictors of the future.

5. _____ An inexperienced person cannot interpret the meaning of Tarot cards.

6. _____ Some psychologists believe that dreams can be valuable in analyzing a person's subconscious issues.

7. _____ If you dream about a rainbow, you will have good fortune.

8. _____ More people reject than accept fortune-telling as a valid way to predict the future.

D. Vocabulary

Complete each of the sentences that follow with the best word from the box. Be sure to use the correct form of the word.

palm	horoscope	reveal	forecast
aspect	analyze	compatible	
subconscious	psychologist	superstition	

1. The _____ believes that his patient has a fear of failing.

2. I want a new roommate. My roommate and I are not _____.

3. She held the coin in the _____ of her hand.

4. The X-ray _____ a broken bone in my arm.

5. My _____ predicts that I am going to be lucky in love.

6. They looked at every _____ of the problem before making a decision.

7. We need to _____ the information before we make a decision.

8. Do you believe in the old _____ that the number 13 is unlucky?

9. The memory of the fire was buried deep in my _____.

10. Warm weather has been _____ for this weekend.

Appendix 1
Word Parts

VOCABULARY SKILLS

A. Word Parts

Many English words are made up of several word parts called **prefixes**, **roots**, and **suffixes**. These parts fit together like pieces of a puzzle.

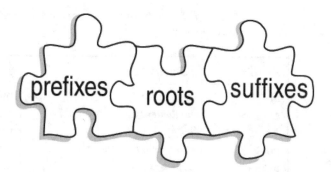

You can increase your vocabulary by learning about the structure of words and how they are formed in English. For example, the word *unfriendly* has three parts. The main part of the word, *friend*, is called the root. The prefix (*un*) and the suffix -ly make *friend* into the word *unfriendly*.

1. Prefixes

One strategy you can use to figure out the meaning of an unfamiliar word is to look at its prefix.

> A **prefix** is a word part that is added to the beginning of a word. A prefix changes the meaning of a word. For example, *dishonest* means "not honest."
> - My ex-husband is a ***dishonest*** man.

2. Negative Prefixes

Some prefixes change a word into its opposite. English has several prefixes that mean *no* or *not*.

Study the following chart to learn some common negative prefixes.

Prefix	Meaning	Example
anti-	*against*	antisocial
dis-	*not*	disobey
il-	*not*	illegal
im-	*not*	impossible
in-	*not*	incorrect
ir-	*not*	irregular
mis-	*wrongly*	misuse
non-	*not*	nonsense
un-	*not*	unable

3. Other Prefixes

Not all prefixes change a word to its opposite, but all prefixes change the word in some way.

Study the following chart to learn some more common prefixes. Learning these prefixes will help you expand your vocabulary.

Prefix	Meaning	Example
bi-	*two, twice*	bilingual, biannual
ex-	*no longer being or doing*	ex-wife, ex-football player
multi-	*many*	multicultural, multicolored
post-	*after, following, later*	postgraduate, postwar
pre-	*before*	prewar, preview
re-	*again, back*	rewrite, redo, rewind
semi-	*half, partly*	semicircle, semiprecious
sub-	*under, below, less important*	substandard, subway, subcommittee
super-	*larger, greater, more powerful*	superhuman, supermarket
trans-	*between two things*	transatlantic, transportation

Appendix 1 Above material from: *Ready to Read Now*

It is easy to discover the meaning of a word and its part of speech if you know common prefixes (word beginnings) and suffixes (word endings).

B. WORD BUILDER 1: PREFIXES AND MEANING

How many prefixes (word beginnings) do you already know? Test your knowledge and then check your answers below. Write the letter of the correct meaning next to each word.

		Prefix	Example	Meaning
1.	C	**ab-**	**ab**sent	a. together
2.	___	**ap-**	**ap**proach	b. not
3.	___	**bene-**	**bene**fit	c. away from
4.	___	**co-**	**co**mmunity	d. to, nearness to
5.	___	**dis-**	**dis**trust	e. good
6.	___	**ex-**	**ex**port	f. one
7.	___	**pre-**	**pre**vious	g. in favor of
8.	___	**pro-**	**pro**pose	h. out
9.	___	**uni-**	**uni**te	i. see
10.	___	**vis-**	**vis**ible	j. before

Answer Key: 1. c, 2. d, 3. e, 4. a, 5. b, 6. h, 7. j, 8. g, 9. f, 10. i

C. WORD BUILDER 2: SUFFIXES AND WORD FAMILIES

How many suffixes (word endings) do you already know? Test your knowledge without looking at the chart that follows.

Suffix	Example	Part of Speech
1. **-able**	*available*	*adj.*
2. **-age**	_____	_____
3. **-al**	_____	_____
4. **-ance**	_____	_____
5. **-ate**	_____	_____
6. **-ation**	_____	_____
7. **-ful**	_____	_____
8. **-ity**	_____	_____
9. **-ize**	_____	_____
10. **-ly**	_____	_____
11. **-ment**	_____	_____
12. **-or**	_____	_____

Suffix Reference Chart: 12 Important Suffixes To Know			
Suffix	Part of Speech	Meaning	Examples From This Book
1. **-able**	adjective	able to	avail**able**, manage**able**
2. **-age**	noun	action	encour**age**, pass**age**
3. **-al**	adjective	like or relating to	critic**al**, tradition**al**
4. **-ance**	noun	act or state of being	insur**ance**, nuis**ance**
5. **-ate**	verb	cause or make	calcul**ate**, migr**ate**
6. **-ation**	noun	act or state of being	gener**ation**, reput**ation**
7. **-ful**	adjective	full of	boast**ful**, grace**ful**
8. **-ity**	noun	state of being	punctual**ity**, van**ity**
9. **-ize**	verb	make	colon**ize**, critic**ize**
10. **-ly**	adverb	like	bitter**ly**, effective**ly**
11. **-ment**	noun	act or result	judg**ment**, require**ment**
12. **-or**	noun	one who	edit**or**, govern**or**

1. Special Uses of Some Suffixes:

-able turns a verb into adjective: drink + **able** = drinkable
                                  verb   adj.

-al turns a noun into an adjective: music + **al** = musical
                                  noun   adj.

-ation turns a verb into a noun: create + **ation** = creation
                                  verb   noun.

-ful turns a noun into an adjective: beauty + **ful** = beautiful
                                  noun   adj.

-ity turns an adjective into a noun: punctual + **ity** = punctuality
                                  adj.   noun

-ment turns a verb into a noun: judge + **ment** = judgment
                                  verb   noun

Appendix 1   Above material from: *Vocabulary Power 2*

Appendix 2

Spelling and Punctuation Rules

It is important to correct spelling errors. This appendix gives you spelling rules, which can assist you in becoming a good speller. It also gives you rules for using apostrophes and for capitalization—two areas related to spelling. Keep this list handy so that you can refer to it while writing.

A. SPELLING RULES FOR WORDS WITH *IE*

This rhyme gives the rule for using i and *e*
> Use i before *e*
> Except after *c*
> Or when sounding like *a*
> As in neighbor and weigh.

Words with *ie*
believe	chief
field	grief

Words with *ei* after *c*
receive	receipt
ceiling	deceit

Words with *ei* sounding like *a*
freight	vein
reign	neighbor

Exceptions
either	neither
leisure	seize
weird	height
foreign	forfeit

B. SPELLING RULES FOR SUFFIXES

When adding -*ing* or another suffix that begins with a vowel or -*y*, drop the final silent -*e*.
> achieve + -*ing* → achieving
> locate + -*ion* → location
> ice + -y → icy

Exceptions

change*able*   notic*eable*

mil*eage*   ey*eing*

When adding *-ing*, change *-ie* to *-y*.

die → d*ying*

tie → t*ying*

lie → l*ying*

When adding a suffix that begins with *a*, consonant, keep the final silent *-e*.

discourage + *-ment* → discourage*ment*

sincere + *-ly* → sincere*ly*

Exceptions

argu*ment*   nin*th*

tru*ly*   who*lly*

When a word ends in a consonant + *-y*, change *-y* to *-i* before adding a suffix.

funny + *-er/-est* → funn*ier*, funn*iest*

try + *-ed* → tr*ied*

allergy + *-ic* → allerg*ic*

Do not make this change if the suffix is *-ing*.

carry → carry*ing*

When a word ends in a vowel + *-y*, keep the *-y*.

delay → delay*ed*

When a word has one syllable and ends in a single vowel + consonant, double the final consonant.

pen → pen*ned*

big → big*ger*, big*gest*

sit → sit*ting*

When a word has more than one syllable and ends in a single vowel + consonant, do not double the final consonant.

happen → happen*ed*

focus → focus*ing*

commit → commit*ment*

C. SPELLING RULES FOR PLURALS

When making most nouns plural, add *-s*.

girl → girl*s*

radio → radio*s*

When a noun ends in *-ch*, *-sh*, *-s*, or *-x*, add *-es*.

church → church*es*

fox → fox*es*

When a noun ends in a consonant + -o, add -es.

   potato → potatoes
   hero → heroes

When a noun ends in a consonant + -y, drop the -y and add -ies.

   lady → ladies
   tragedy → tragedies

D. SPELLING RULES FOR PREFIXES

Add a prefix to the beginning of a word without doubling or dropping letters.

   satisfy → *dis*satisfy
   behave → *mis*behave
   natural → *un*natural

E. CAPITALIZATION RULES

Rules for capitalization include the following:

1. Capitalize the first word of each sentence.

2. Capitalize proper nouns (nouns that name specific people, places, groups, and things, including languages, and religious, ethnic, and political groups).

   Adeline Yen Mah, Vancouver, Spanish, Moslems, Hispanic, Democrats

3. Capitalize adjectives of nationality and regional or religious affiliation.

   Brazilian restaurant, Basque region, Christian church

4. Capitalize titles before proper names.

   Professor William Su, Reverend Hoffman, Uncle Joe

5. Capitalize important words in titles of books, plays, movies, newspapers, magazines, songs, etc.

   Romeo and Juliet, The Sound of Music, The Daily Mirror, Newsweek

6. Capitalize historical events and periods.

   Korean War, the Cold War, Renaissance

7. Capitalize holidays, days, and months.

   Easter, Monday, January

8. Do not capitalize seasons.

   summer, spring, winter, fall/autumn

F. APOSTROPHE RULES

1. Use an apostrophe to show one or more letters have been left out.

   cannot → can't

   that is → that's

   we are → we're

2. Use an apostrophe to show ownership.

   the book of the student → the student's book

   the home of James → James's home

   the offices of the professors → the professors' offices

Appendix 3
Punctuation Rules

Using correct punctuation is important because punctuation conveys meaning just as words do. Consider these two sentences:

> Eat children.
> Eat, children.

Both sentences are commands, but the first sentence would be correct only in a society of cannibals[1]! Learn and practice the rules of punctuation until you are confident about using them correctly.

A. COMMAS[2]

Commas are sometimes troublesome to learners of English because they are used differently in other languages. There are many comma rules in English, but you may remember them more easily if you realize that they can be organized into just four main groups: **introducers, coordinators, inserters,** and **tags.** Each group of commas relates to independent clauses in a particular way, except the coordinator group. Coordinator commas link not just independent clauses but *any* coordinate (equal) elements in a sentence.

Study the examples for each comma group, and notice the kinds of elements that can be introducers, coordinators, inserters, and tags.

1. Introducer Commas

An introducer comma follows any element that comes in front of the first independent clause in a sentence.

	Therefore, I plan to quit smoking.
	Nervously, I threw away my cigarettes.
WORDS	**As a result,** I feel terrible right now.
	After 16 years of smoking, it is not easy to quit.
PHRASES	**Having smoked for 16 years,** I find it difficult to quit.

[1]*cannibals*: people who eat human flesh
[2]Thanks to Anne Katz of ARC Associates, Oakland, California, for permission to adapt her presentation of comma rules.

DEPENDENT CLAUSES	**Because I have a chronic cough,** my doctor recommended that I quit immediately.
DIRECT QUOTATIONS	**"Stop smoking today,"** she advised.

2. Coordinator Commas

Together with a coordinating conjunction, a comma links coordinate (equal) elements in a sentence.

COMPOUND SENTENCE WITH 2 INDEPENDENT CLAUSES	**She has a good job,** yet **she is always broke**. **They were tired,** so **they went home early**.
SERIES OF 3 OR MORE WORDS	He does not enjoy **skiing, ice-skating,** or **sledding**. Cecille speaks **English, Spanish, French,** and **Creole**. (*No comma with only two items: Chen speaks Mandarin and Taiwanese.*)
SERIES OF 3 OR MORE PHRASES	A nurse has to work **at night, on weekends,** and **on holidays**. We **ran into the airport, checked our luggage, raced to the boarding gate, gave the attendant our boarding passes,** and **collapsed in our seats**.

3. Inserter Commas

An inserter comma is used before and after any element that is inserted into the middle of an independent clause.

WORDS	My uncle, **however,** refuses to quit smoking.
PHRASES	My father, **on the other hand,** has never smoked. There is no point in living, **according to my uncle,** if you do not do what you enjoy.
NONRESTRICTIVE PHRASES AND CLAUSES	My aunt, **his wife,** died of lung cancer. My cousins, **grieving over their mother's death,** resolved never to smoke. My mother, **who just celebrated her fiftieth birthday,** enjoys an occasional cigarette.
REPORTING VERBS IN DIRECT QUOTATIONS	"I have tried to quit dozens of times," **she says,** "but I can't."

4. Tag Commas

A tag comma is used when adding certain elements to the end of a sentence.

WORDS	My uncle believes in drinking a daily glass of wine, **too.**[3] He appears to be in good health, **however**.
PHRASES	He swims for an hour every day, **for example**. He also plays tennis, **beating me most of the time**.
TAG QUESTIONS	It is not logical, **is it**?
DIRECT QUOTATIONS	He laughs as he says, **"I will outlive all of you."**

[3]Many writers do not use a comma before *too*.

Appendix 3 Above material from: *Writing Academic English Level 4, Fourth Edition*

Apendix 4

Connecting Words and Transition Signals

A. COORDINATING WORDS

1. Coordinating Conjunctions

Coordinating conjunctions connect grammatically equal elements. Coordinating conjunctions are sometimes called the "Fan Boys" conjunctions—For, And, Nor, But, Or, Yet, So.

Conjunction	Function	Example
for	Connects a reason to a result	I am a little hungry, **for** I didn't eat breakfast this morning.
and	Connects equal similar ideas	John likes to fish **and** hunt.
nor	Connects two negative sentences	She does not eat meat, **nor** does she drink milk.
but	Connects equal different ideas	I like to eat fish **but** not to catch them.
or	Connects two equal choices	Do you prefer coffee **or** tea?
yet	Connects equal contrasting ideas	It is sunny **yet** cold.
so	Connects a result to a reason	I did not eat breakfast this morning, **so** I am a little hungry.

2. Paired (Correlative) Conjunctions

Correlative conjunctions are always in pairs. Like coordinating conjunctions, they connect grammatically equal elements.

Conjunction Pairs	Example
both . . . and	**Both** San Francisco **and** Sydney have beautiful harbors.
not only . . . but also	Japanese food is **not only** delicious to eat **but also** beautiful to look at.
either . . . or	Bring **either** a raincoat **or** an umbrella when you visit Seattle.
neither . . . nor	My grandfather could **neither** read **nor** write, but he was a very wise person.
whether . . . or	The newlyweds could not decide **whether** to live with her parents **or** to rent an apartment.

B. SUBORDINATING WORDS

A subordinating word is the first word in a dependent clause. Common subordinating words include the following.

Subordinating Conjunctions for Adverb Clauses

Time (When?)	
after	**After** we ate lunch, we decided to go shopping.
as, just as	**Just as** we left the house, it started to rain.
as long as	We waited **as long as** we could.
as soon as	**As soon as** the front door closed, I looked for my house key.
before	I thought I had put it in my coat pocket **before** we left.
since	I have not locked myself out of the house **since** I was 10 years old.
until	**Until** I was almost 12, my mother pinned the key to my coat.
when	**When** I turned 12, my mother let me keep the key in my pocket.
whenever	I usually put the key in the same place **whenever** I come home.
while	**While** I searched for the key, it rained harder and harder.

Place (Where?)	
where	I like to shop **where** prices are low.
wherever	I try to shop **wherever** there is a sale.
anywhere	You can find bargains **anywhere** you shop.
everywhere	I use my credit card **everywhere** I shop.
Manner (How?)	
as, just as	I love to get flowers(,) **as** most women do.*
as if	You look **as if** you didn't sleep at all last night.
as though	She acts **as though** she doesn't know us.
Distance (How far? How near? How close?)	
as + *adverb* + as	We will hike **as far as** we can before it turns dark.
	The child sat **as close as** she could to her mother.
	The child sat **as close** to her mother **as** she could.
Frequency (How often?)	
as often as	I call my parents **as often as** I can.
Reason (Why?)	
as	I can't take evening classes(,) **as** I work at night.*
because	I can't take evening classes **because** I work at night.
since	I can't take evening classes **since** I work at night.
Purpose (For what purpose?)	
so that	Many people emigrate **so that** their children can have a better life.
in order that	Many people emigrate **in order that** their children can have a better life.
Result (With what result?)	
so + *adjective* + that	I was **so tired** last night **that** I fell asleep at dinner.
so + *adverb* + that	She talks **so softly that** the other students cannot hear her.
such a(n) + *noun* + that	It was **such an easy test that** most of the students got A's.
so much/many/little/few + *noun* + that	He is taking **so many classes that** he has no time to sleep.

*This is an exception to the usual rule for commas. Many writers use a comma before *as*.

Condition (Under what condition?)	
if	We will not go hiking **if** it rains.
unless	We will not go hiking **unless** the weather is perfect.
Partial Contrast	
although	I love my brother **although** we disagree about almost everything.
even though	I love my brother **even though** we disagree about almost everything.
though	I love my brother **though** we disagree about almost everything.
Contrast (Direct opposites)	
while	My brother likes classical music, **while** I prefer hard rock.
whereas	He dresses conservatively, **whereas** I like to be a little shocking.

Subordinating Words for Adjective Clauses

To Refer to People	
who, whom, whose, that (informal)	People **who** live in glass houses should not throw stones.
	My parents did not approve of the man **whom** my sister married.
	An orphan is a child **whose** parents are dead.
To Refer to Animals and Things	
which	My new computer, **which** I bought yesterday, stopped working today.
that	Yesterday I received an e-mail **that** I did not understand.
To Refer to a Time or a Place	
when	Thanksgiving is a time **when** families travel great distances to be together.
where	An orphanage is a place **where** orphans live.

Appendix 4 Above material from: *Writing Academic English Level 4, Fourth Edition*

Subordinating Words for Noun Clauses

That Clauses	
that	Do you believe **that** there is life in outer space?

If/Whether Clauses	
whether	I can't remember **whether** I locked the door.
whether or not	**whether or not** I locked the door.
whether . . . or not	**whether** I locked the door **or not**.
if	I can't remember **if** I locked the door.
if . . . or not	**if** I locked the door **or not**.

Question Clauses	
who, whoever, whom	**Whoever** arrives at the bus station first should buy the tickets.
which, what, where	Do you know **where** the bus station is?
when, why, how	We should ask **when** the bus arrives.
how much, how many	Do not worry about **how much** they cost.
how long, how often, etc.	He didn't care **how long** he had to wait.

Notice that some subordinating conjunctions can introduce different kinds of dependent clauses. *That* can introduce either noun clauses or adjective clauses, and *where* can introduce either a noun, an adjective, or an adverb clause. It normally is not important to know the kind of clause.

> I can't remember **where** I put the house key. (noun clause; direct object of *remember*)

> It's not in the place **where** I usually put it. (adjective clause; tells *which place*)

> I always put it **where** I will see it when I go out the front door. (adverb clause; tells *where I put it*)

C. Conjunctive Adverbs

Conjunctive adverbs can appear at the beginning, in the middle, or at the end of one independent clause, but we often use them to connect two independent clauses.

Remember to put a semicolon before and a comma after the conjunctive adverb if an independent clause follows.

Conjunctive Adverb	Examples
To add a similar idea	
also	Community colleges offer preparation for many jobs; **also,** they prepare students to transfer to four-year colleges or universities.
besides	; **besides,**
furthermore	; **furthermore,**
in addition	; **in addition,**
moreover	; **moreover,**
To add an unexpected or surprising continuation	
however	The cost of attending a community college is low; **however,** many students need financial aid.
nevertheless	; **nevertheless,**
nonetheless	; **nonetheless,**
still	; **still,**
To add a complete contrast	
in contrast	Most community colleges do not have dormitories; **in contrast,** most four-year colleges do.
on the other hand	; **on the other hand,**
To add a result	
as a result	Native and nonnative English speakers have different needs; **as a result,** most schools provide separate classes for each group.
consequently	; **consequently,**
therefore	; **therefore,**
thus	; **thus,**

Appendix 4   Above material from: *Writing Academic English Level 4, Fourth Edition*

To list ideas in order of time	
meanwhile	Police kept people away from the scene of the accident; **meanwhile**, ambulance workers tried to pull victims out of the wreck.
afterward	The workers put five injured people into an ambulance; **afterward**, they found another victim.
then	; **then**,
subsequently	; **subsequently**,

To give an example	
for example	Colors can have different meanings; **for example**, white is the color of weddings in some cultures and of funerals in others.
for instance	; **for instance**,

To show similarities	
similarly	Hawaii has sunshine and friendly people; **similarly**, Mexico's weather is sunny and its people hospitable.
likewise	; **likewise**,

To indicate "the first statement is not true; the second statement is true"	
instead	The medicine did not make him feel better; **instead**, it made him feel worse.
on the contrary	; **on the contrary**,
rather	; **rather**,
instead (meaning "as a substitute")	They had planned to go to Hawaii on their honeymoon; **instead**, they went to Mexico.

To give another possibility	
on the other hand	You can live in a dorm on campus; **on the other hand**, you can rent a room with a family off campus.
alternatively	; **alternatively**,
otherwise (meaning "if not")	Students must take final exams; **otherwise**, they will receive a grade of Incomplete.

To add an explanation	
in other words	Some cultures are matriarchal; **in other words,** the mothers are the head of the family.
that is	; that is,
To make a stronger statement	
indeed	Mangoes are a very common fruit; **indeed,** people eat more mangoes than any other fruit in the world.
in fact	; in fact,

D. TRANSITION SIGNALS

Transition Signals and Conjunctive Adverbs	Coordinating Conjunctions and Paired Conjunctions	Subordinating Conjunctions	Others: Adjectives, Prepositions, Verbs
To list ideas in order of time			
first, . . .		before	the first (reason, cause, step, etc.)
first of all, . . .		after	the second . . .
second, . . .		until	the third . . .
third, . . .		when	another . . .
next, . . .		while	the last . . .
then . . .		as soon as	the final . . .
after that, . . .		since	
meanwhile, . . .			
in the meantime, . . .			
finally, . . .			
last, . . .			
last of all, . . .			
subsequently, . . .			

Appendix 4   Above material from: *Writing Academic English Level 4, Fourth Edition*

To list ideas in order of importance			
first, . . .			the first . . . (reason, cause, step, etc.)
first of all, . . .			an additional . . .
first and foremost, . . .			the second . . .
second, . . .			another . . .
more important, . . .			a more important (reason, cause, step, etc.)
most important, . . .			
more significantly, . . .			the most important . . .
most significantly, . . .			
above all, . . .			the most significant . . .
most of all, . . .			the best/the worst . . .
To add a similar or equal idea			
also, . . .	and		another . . . (reason, cause, step, etc.)
besides, . . .	both . . . and		a second . . .
furthermore, . . .	not only . . . but also		an additional . . .
in addition, . . .			a final . . .
moreover, . . .			as well as
too			
as well			
To add an opposite idea			
however, . . .	but	although	despite
on the other hand, . . .	yet	even though	in spite of
nevertheless, . . .		though	
nonetheless, . . .			
still, . . .			

To explain or restate an idea			
in other words, . . . in particular, . . . (more) specifically, . . . that is, . . .			

To make a stronger statement			
indeed, . . . in fact, . . .			

To give another possibility			
alternatively, . . . on the other hand, . . . otherwise, . . .	or either . . . or whether . . . or		

To give an example			
for example, . . . for instance, . . .			such as an example of to exemplify

To express an opinion			
according to . . . in my opinion, . . . in my view, . . .			to believe (that) to feel (that) to think (that)

To give a reason			
for this reason, . . .	for	because	as a result of because of due to

Appendix 4   Above material from: *Writing Academic English Level 4, Fourth Edition*

To give a result			
accordingly, . . .	so		the cause of
as a consequence, . . .			the reason for
as a result, . . .			to cause
consequently, . . .			to result (in)
for these reasons, . . .			to have an effect on
hence, . . .			to affect
therefore, . . .			
thus, . . .			

To add a conclusion			
all in all, . . .			
in brief, . . .			
in short, . . .			
to conclude, . . .			
to summarize, . . .			
in conclusion, . . .			
in summary, . . .			
for these reasons, . . .			

To show similarities			
likewise, . . .	and		alike, like, just like
similarly, . . .	both . . . and		as, just as
also	not only . . . but also		as well
	neither . . . nor		as well as
			compared with or to
			in comparison with or to
			to be similar (to) too

To show differences			
however, . . .			instead of
in contrast, . . .			
instead, . . .			
on the contrary, . . .			
on the other hand, . . .			
rather, . . .			

Appendix 4   Above material from: *Writing Academic English Level 4, Fourth Edition*

Process Essay

Read this passage and underline the sequence signal words. Then turn the page and try to remember the steps in the process of making a submarine sandwich.

Hot Subs for Lunch

The name may be different in other parts of the world. But in Boston, they are known as "subs," or submarine sandwiches. Their name is due to their shape, long and narrow like a submarine. A sub sandwich is one of the most popular lunch items in town.

The best way to find out about subs is to go to a sub shop. There, these delicious treats are a specialty. You will find huge ovens right behind the counter, because a real sub is served hot.

You wait in line until it is your turn to place your order. The sub sandwich maker usually begins by asking, "What kind of sub do you want?" You might answer, "Large Italian," and the expert goes to work.

First, he takes a large, long bread roll from a plastic bag under the counter. He slices it lengthwise and puts in layers of meat and cheese. For the Italian sub, he'd include Genoa salami, mortadella sausage, other cold meats, and Provolone cheese.

Next, leaving the sandwich open, the sandwich chef places it on a metal tray and slides it into the hot oven. He bakes it until the meat is warm and the roll is toasty. When the cheese has melted a bit, he knows it's time to take it out. Then he calls out, "What do you want on your large Italian?"

When you reply, "Everything," he adds mayonnaise, salt, pepper, olive oil, and a sprinkling of oregano. But that is not all. He also puts in lots of chopped pickles, onions, and hot peppers. Then he tops it off with sliced tomatoes and crunchy chopped iceberg lettuce.

Finally, taking the sandwich in his hand, the sandwich maker folds the two sides together. He carefully cuts it in half and wraps the finished product in waxed paper.

"For here or to go?" he asks. No matter where you eat it, you can be sure that you will enjoy lunch that day!

What are the steps in the process of making a submarine sandwich? They are listed below, but they are out of order. On the lines below, number the steps in the correct order. Do not look back. Then, working with another student, explain how to make a sub sandwich. Remember to use sequence signal words.

a. _____ He piles sliced meat and cheese on it.

b. _____ He adds mayonnaise, salt, pepper, and lots more.

c. _____ He places it on a metal tray.

d. _____ He wraps it in waxed paper.

e. _____ He folds the two sides together.

f. ___1___ He takes a large, long bread roll from a plastic bag.

g. _____ He slices the roll in half lengthwise.

h. _____ He asks, "For here or to go?"

i. _____ He calls out, "What do you want on your large Italian?"

j. _____ He allows it to bake until the meat is warm.

Read the following paragraph. Notice that the author has used a sequence pattern. On the lines below, write the main idea, the signal words, and the steps or events. Compare your work with that of another student.

Main Idea: _____

_____

Signal Words   **Steps**

_____   _____

_____   _____

_____   _____

_____   _____

Tires are one part of the car that need a lot of attention. You need, of course, to check the amount of air in the tire and the amount of wear on the surface of the tire. But that is not enough. You should also bring your car regularly to the mechanic or tire specialist for some other work. First, the mechanic should rotate the tires after a certain number of miles. This means that the tires are removed and then put back on in a different position. The rear tires, for example, are usually moved to the front. The front tires are then moved to the rear and exchanged. That is, the tire that had been on the left front is now on the right rear and the tire that had been on the right front is now on the left rear. Changing the tires like this will prevent them from becoming too worn on one side. For this same reason, the mechanic should also balance the wheels. In balancing the wheels, each wheel is taken off and adjusted to make sure it goes around evenly.

On a separate sheet of paper, write a paragraph that uses the sequence pattern and begins with one of the main idea statements below. Complete the paragraph with sentences describing events or steps. To guide your reader, use sequence signal words for each event or step.

1. Main Idea Statements

1. It's easy to make a cup of tea.

2. A trip to another country requires a lot of planning.

3. Learning how to play _____ is a long process. (Add the name of a sport.)

After you have written your paragraph, ask another student to read it. Find out if your ideas were clear and interesting. Then rewrite the paragraph to include any suggestions from your partner.

Modals

Check your understanding of modals. Put a check (✓) next to the sentences that are correct.

1. _____ Jim should gives his mother a nice gift on Mother's Day.

2. _____ Last semester I had to write three essays in one night because I put them off until the last minute.

3. _____ Mozart was a child prodigy; he can play the piano at a very young age.

4. _____ If you want an A, you can study tonight.

5. _____ This book may be the best one I have ever read.

6. _____ Your mom didn't know where you were, but she said you might be next door.

7. _____ I'm not sure, but I think we are suppose to leave tonight.

8. _____ It snowed so much yesterday that we not able to drive home.

9. _____ Lonnie is so sick that she had better see a doctor soon.

10. _____ I want to offer you a job at my restaurant. I may pay you minimum wage plus tips.

A. EDITING FOCUS

Modals are auxiliary verbs. They are used with main verbs to give advice and to express ideas like ability, necessity, or possibility. Examples of modals are *can*, *might*, and *should*. Most modals have more than one meaning. For example, *can* is used for possibility, ability, and permission.

Phrasal modals are expressions with meanings similar to those of modal auxiliaries. They include expressions like *be able to*, *be supposed to*, and *have to*. As writer and editor of your writing, you need to make sure that you use the correct forms of modals and phrasal modals to express the meaning you want to convey.

1. Forming Modals

Present/Future Time

1. Modal auxiliaries have only one form. Use a modal + the base form of the verb. The base form of the verb is used with all subjects. Do not add -s to the base form for third person singular subjects. For negative statements, put *not* after the modal.

	Affirmative: modal + base form of verb		**Negative: modal + not + base form of verb**	
I You He, She, It We You They	can could will would should ought to may might must had better	+ eat	I You He, She, It We You They	cannot* could not will not would not should not ** may not might not must not had better not	+ eat

Cannot is written as one word.
**Americans do not usually use the negative of *ought to*. Use *shouldn't* instead.

He **may need** more time to finish his paper.
NOT
He may needs more time to finish his paper.

He **had better not** drive because there won't be anywhere to park.
NOT
He had not better drive because there won't be anywhere to park.

2. Although modals do not change form with different subjects, phrasal modals with *be* and *have* do change form to agree with the subject.

I **am supposed to** practice today.

Michael **has to** help his parents move.

John and Kim **are able** to do the homework.

Appendix 6   Above material from: *Eye on Editing 1*

3. To make questions and negatives with *have to*, use *do, does, do not,* or *does not.*

   What **do** I **have to** do to get a visa?

   Does he **have to** make an appointment to see her?

   I **don't have to** finish my essay until Friday.

   Maria **doesn't have to** go to class tomorrow.

Past Time

The following are the past tense forms for some modals and phrasal modals.

Present	Past
can	could
have to/has to	had to
am/is/are/able to	was/were able to
am/is/are supposed to	was/were supposed to

When I was a child, I **could** play the violin.

We **had to** call a tow truck to pull the car out of the ditch.

Their plane **wasn't able to** take off because of the snowstorm.

We **were supposed to** call home as soon as we arrived, but we forgot.

Self Check 1

Correct the errors in modal forms.

1. Financial aid can helps many students continue their education.

2. Desert communities has to start water conservation programs soon.

3. You should study not with the television on.

4. Robert have to prepare to give a presentation.

5. Has Pat to go to the library to do the research?

2. Using Modals

Meaning	Present	Future	Past
Showing Ability	can am/is/are able to She **can** play the piano very well.	can am/is/are able to	could was/were able to
Making Requests	can could would **Would** you please proofread this essay for me?	can could would will	
Showing Possibility	can may might could I **might** take an art class next semester.	can may might could	
Showing Near Certainty (deduction)	must His office door is locked; he **must** not be here today.	—	
Asking for and Giving Permission	can could may **May** I borrow this book from you? Sure you can.	can could may	
Showing Necessity	must has/have to You **must** arrive by 10:15 A.M.	must has/have to	had to
Showing Prohibition	must not cannot You **cannot** talk during the exam.	must not cannot	
Showing Lack of Necessity	do/does not + have to You **do not have to** type the outline for your paper.	do/does not + have to	did not have to
Giving Advice/Making Suggestions	had better (not) am/is/are supposed to should ought to can could You **should** visit your professor during her office hours for some help.	had better (not) am/is/are supposed to should ought to can could	was supposed to

Note: For a comprehensive list of past tense modals, refer to a grammar book.

Appendix 6   Above material from: *Eye on Editing 1*

Self Check 2

Correct the errors in modal use.

1. You might not talk to other students during the exam.

2. You had better turn in the essay late or you will fail the course.

3. You must not take a final exam if you don't want to; you can write a research paper instead.

4. Cats may climb trees and see in the dark.

5. The office door is locked and the lights are off; they should be closed today.

> **Tip**
> Read your essay out loud several times. Sometimes it's easy to hear grammar errors that your eyes miss during silent reading.

B. Editing Practice

Put a check (✓) next to the sentences that use modals correctly. Correct the sentences that have errors.

1. _____ I know you're busy, so you are not supposed to do the dishes if you don't have time.

2. _____ Diane better pass the test, or she may fail the class.

3. _____ Ava is supposed to turn in her paper a day early.

4. _____ I have a cellular phone, so now he can calls me wherever I go.

5. _____ Can you offer my son a job?

6. _____ You must not ever to call her again.

7. _____ When we first arrived at the airport, we cannot find a place to park.

8. _____ The Nelson family cannot afford to take a vacation this year.

9. _____ John could not come to the game last night because he has to work.

10. _____ You should not talk on the phone and drive at the same time because it is dangerous.

In the following paragraph, seven of the underlined modal and verb combinations are not correct. Find and correct the errors.

As we know, we will probably find many differences between schools in a foreign country and schools in the United States. One big difference between Asian and American schools is that in Asian schools the students (1) <u>must stand</u> when the teacher enters the classroom. When I was a student in an Asian school, we (2) <u>have to bow</u> every time a teacher entered. To most Americans, this form of respect (3) <u>must looking</u> strange, and this behavior (4) <u>may seems</u> unusual. Also in my culture, parents and teachers force children to study because they believe the children (5) <u>can not make</u> the decision to study for themselves. Punishment is a common form of motivation in Eastern schools. In my primary school, when we didn't work hard we (6) <u>were supposed to receive</u> a painful slap on the hand. At that time punishment was normal to me, and I think it probably gave me the discipline to work hard in school. When my family and I came to the United States, we (7) <u>has to adapt</u> to a very different educational style. It is still hard for me to believe that physical punishment is illegal in American schools. Now I enjoy the fact that I (8) <u>would learn</u> my lessons on my own and not because a teacher or parent is forcing me. After being educated in two countries, I would like my children to receive a combination of both educational styles. I hope they (9) <u>must see</u> the benefits from the educational traditions of both cultures.

Underline the modals in the following sentences. In your own words, write the meaning of each sentence in the blank. Use a modal different from the one in the sentence to express the meaning, or give the meaning without using a modal.

Example: You <u>have to</u> put the stamp in the upper right-hand corner of the envelope.

Meaning: <u>*It is necessary to put the stamp in the upper right-hand corner of the envelope.*</u>

1. Arman, Isabel, and Ali may go out for dinner tonight.

   Meaning: _____

2. In class today, my instructor said we have to read the whole textbook this quarter.

   Meaning: _____

3. I should learn to speak a second language, but I do not have much free time.

   Meaning: _____

4. Tourists can eat a lot of delicious food on a vacation in Italy.

   Meaning: _____

5. Marcus must learn how to swim before he takes the scuba diving class.

   Meaning: _____

Underline the ten modal and verb combinations used in this essay. Six have errors. Find and correct the errors. There may be more than one way to correct some errors.

In the novel *Black Boy*, by Richard Wright, the author writes about his own life. Throughout the novel Richard Wright is a very independent person. This may be because Richard's father leaves the family when Richard is still a boy. Therefore, Richard is able to be responsible for doing the household chores and taking care of his younger brother. Richard also have to stand up for himself, which is often difficult for a child. Even though

         Appendix 6   Above material from: *Eye on Editing 1*

he experiences hardship as a child, Richard is able to maintain his curiosity and interest in life. Later, more unhappiness comes to Richard and his family. His mother has a stroke and is partially paralyzed. Richard is forced to take help from the neighbors. Soon after, Richard's grandmother comes to help the family. She must look after Richard's mother and brother better than Richard can. Later, other relatives arrive and decide that Grandmother is able not to watch Richard's family any longer. After his grandmother leaves, Richard has to live with his Uncle Edward, and Richard's brother goes to live with his Aunt Maggie.

I liked reading this novel about Richard Wright and how he reacts to racial issues in America. The story may helps readers understand issues that African Americans face in the United States. I prefer learning history through a novel like *Black Boy* to learning through history books. Studying books like *Black Boy* might encourage students to explore complex issues with interest and passion. I can not forget the lessons I learned about racism and hardship from this novel.

C. WRITING TOPICS

Choose one of the topics and write at least one paragraph. Use a variety of modals. After you complete your first draft, concentrate on editing your work. Keep in mind the editing practice from this chapter.

1. What should or must each of us do to make the world a better and safer place to live? What could each of us do to help reduce problems like racism, pollution, or violence?

2. The norms that children must follow are different from the ones adults must follow. What are some rules that children must follow, and what are others that adults have to follow? What could you do as a child that you are not allowed to do now? What can you do now that you were not supposed to do as a child?

Gerunds and Infinitives

Check your understanding of verb forms, gerunds, and infinitives. Put a check (✓) next to the sentences that are correct.

1. _____ Are you interested in going to the play-off game this weekend?

2. _____ They avoid to drive at rush hour.

3. _____ Emily loves to read nineteenth-century English literature.

4. _____ Please don't make me to practice anymore.

5. _____ Johnnie is accustomed to studying late at night.

6. _____ Mr. Tang plans to go on a cruise to Cuba from Mexico.

7. _____ I miss to see my family.

A. GERUNDS AND INFINITIVES

In addition to the five basic forms, verbs in English also have a gerund form (verb + -*ing*) and an infinitive form (*to* + verb). In these forms, however, the verb no longer acts as a verb. Gerunds and infinitives act as nouns—either as subjects, as objects of verbs and prepositions, or as complements.

1. Verb + Gerund or Infinitive

Some verbs can take either gerunds or infinitives as their objects. These verbs include the following:

begin	continue	hate	like	love	prefer	start

She **hates** *swimming*/*to swim* in the ocean.
They**'ve loved** *reading*/*to read* since they were children.
We **preferred** *studying* /**to study** on the fourth floor of the library last year.

2. Verb + Gerund

Some verbs can take gerunds but not infinitives as their objects. These verbs include the following:

appreciate	delay	dislike	finish	mention	miss	suggest
avoid	discuss	enjoy	keep	mind	quit	

I **avoid** *working* out at the gym.
Aaron **dislikes** *traveling* by bus.
Susan **suggested** *seeing* the new ballet at Lincoln Center.

3. Verb + Infinitive

Some verbs take an infinitive or a noun + infinitive, but cannot take a gerund as their object. These verbs include the following:

advise	encourage	intend	order	seem
agree	expect	invite	plan	tell
ask	force	learn	pretend	want
decide	hope	offer	remind	warn

Susan **agreed** *to go* with him to a concert.
The university **requires** potential students **to write** an essay.

> **Tip**
> If you are unsure whether a verb is followed by an infinitive or a gerund, a grammar book can give you this information.

4. Preposition + Gerund

- *Prepositions such as in, on, by, for, with, etc., can be followed by gerunds but not infinitives.*
  He made up an excuse **for** *arriving* late to dinner.

- *Two-word verbs and other verb + preposition combinations can also be followed by gerunds but not infinitives.*
  I often **put off** *studying* until right before a test.
  I am **accustomed to** *studying* until 1:00 A.M.
  Have you **thought about** *going* to graduate school?

Common two-word verbs followed by gerunds include:

give up	insist on	keep on	put off

Other common verb + preposition combinations followed by gerunds include:

apologize for	complain about	look forward to	prohibit (someone) from	talk about
believe in	insist on	plan on	take care of	think about

Common be + adjective + preposition combinations followed by gerunds include:

be accustomed to	be excited about	be preoccupied with	be worried about
be bored with	be interested in	be tired of	

> **Tip**
> Be careful! Do not confuse the preposition *to* (in *be accustomed to, look forward to*, etc.) with the *to* used in the infinitive (*to go, to be*, etc.). The preposition *to* is followed by a gerund. The infinitive *to* is followed by the base form of the verb.

5. Verb + Base Form

The verbs *make, have, let*, and *help* can all be used to write about causing someone to do something or making it possible for someone to do something. Used this way, these words are followed by a noun phrase or pronoun + the base form of a verb. *Help* can be followed by an infinitive instead of a base form.

The coach **made us run** another lap, and then he **had us do** more push-ups.
She **lets her daughter go out** on dates.
Can you **help me (to) paint** the house?

Self Check 3

Correct the errors involving verbs with gerunds, infinitives, or base forms.

1. Healthy eaters dislike to eat a lot of sugar.

2. He hopes to seeing a Broadway show in New York.

3. The hike made them felt tired all day.

4. They are excited about join the club.

5. I look forward to swim in the lake this summer.

> **Tip**
> Edit your writing on a printed copy rather than on the computer screen. Editing is much more thorough and accurate on paper.

B. EDITING PRACTICE

Put a check (✓) next to the sentences that use verb forms, gerunds, and infinitives correctly. Correct the sentences that have errors.

1. _____ The counselor advised us to begin the university application process early.

2. _____ Negligent pet owners let their animals to wander the streets.

3. _____ Mr. Gong made his son play the violin.

4. _____ Some people believe criticism helps children behaving appropriately.

5. _____ The Berlin Wall doesn't divides East and West Germany anymore.

6. _____ Mrs. Hasam suggested taking a charter flight because it was less expensive.

7. _____ I love the sound when the wind is blow through the trees.

8. _____ The San Francisco campus cover three hundred acres of land.

9. _____ Has the principal being to your house?

10. _____ I apologized for losing Anthony's book.

11. _____ I didn't found the ring I lost last week.

12. _____ The students look forward to finish the project.

In the following paragraph, the underlined verbs are not correct. Write the correct verb form above each underlined verb phrase.

For many people, personal health and healthcare are important parts of their lives. A common way to deal with health issues is through diet and exercise. On average, the typical person (1) <u>is live</u> longer than in the past but not necessarily in a healthier way. Many people (2) <u>dislike to make</u> lifestyle changes even though the changes (3) <u>may making</u> them feel better in old age. People (4) <u>do not likes</u> to sacrifice now for uncertain benefits in the future. However, if problems such as obesity and high blood pressure are not controlled, a majority of sufferers (5) <u>will developing</u> heart disease in the future. More women than men exercise regularly and (6) <u>have improve</u> their eating habits. However, there are probably few differences between men's and women's health. The main difference is between people who (7) <u>decide eating</u> a healthy, well-balanced diet and those who (8) <u>let themselves to become</u> lazy when it comes to food. This goes for exercise as well. Even though the number one health concern for most people is weight, and many (9) <u>are preoccupied with lose weight</u>, obesity rates continue to rise. A healthy diet makes one (10) <u>enjoy to exercise more</u>, and a moderate amount of exercise (11) <u>helps people eating</u> well. Therefore, both are necessary for maintaining a healthy lifestyle. It's ironic that in the past people (12) <u>did not worried</u> as much as we do today about living healthy lives, yet their health was probably better than ours.

Read the following paragraph. Complete the paragraph with the correct form of each verb given.

In the United States during World War II, many Japanese Americans were sent to internment camps.[1] These Americans did not _____ why they

1. understand

were being treated as criminals; however, the U.S. government believed that Japanese Americans might _____ American secrets to Japan. Many

2. give

[1]**internment camps:** areas where prisoners are held, especially during war

Appendix 7 Above material from: *Eye on Editing 1*

Japanese Americans were sent to a camp called Manzanar. Government and camp offi-

cials did not _____ the camp residents _____

3. help   4. adapt

to their new surroundings. The Japanese Americans were on their own and could

only _____ for an improved situation. As the U.S. involvement

5. hope

in World War II was _____, the government let the internees[2]

6. end

_____ to U.S. locations farther east. After the war had finally

7. move

_____, Japanese Americans were forced _____

8. end   9. leave

the camps. They began _____ about resuming their shattered lives.

10. think

Over the past decades, other Americans have slowly been learning more about this

episode in U.S. history and are interested in _____ to correct past

11. try

wrongs. Thinking about past injustices reminds us _____ these

12. prevent

kinds of actions before they happen again.

The following paragraph has ten errors in the use of verb forms, gerunds, and infinitives. Find and correct the errors.

Los Angeles is a city that is full of excitement and diversity. It is unfortunate that the city has receive a lot of bad press because of the smog, the crime, and the riots in the early 1990s. Although some negative perceptions of Los Angeles may be accurate, tourists should not to overlook the city when they make their travel plans. In fact, southern California residents ought to think about visit downtown more often. This area has becomes a center of excitement and diversity. Koreatown, Little Tokyo, and Olvera Street all exist within several square miles of each other. This racial diversity helps Angelenos understanding other cultures and beliefs and in addition, helps them accepting differences more easily. The city's art community is also first-rate. Previously, Los Angeles did not had a theater district like New York City does, but now there are several theater complexes and many small theaters throughout the city. The one thing Los Angeles has always being famous for is Hollywood, and it's better than ever. Hollywood is responsible for entertain the world and, like the rest of the city, promises to impressing visitors and residents alike.

[2]**internees:** people in internment camps, prisoners

Appendix 8
Using a Dictionary

Dictionaries are full of information that will help you learn, understand, and use English correctly.

1. Guidewords

The words in a dictionary are listed in alphabetical order. To find words quickly, you should use the guidewords at the top of each dictionary page. Look at the pages below. The guideword *brotherly* in the left corner is the first word on the left page. The guideword *bug* in the right corner is the last word on the right page. Using guidewords will help you to find a word quickly.

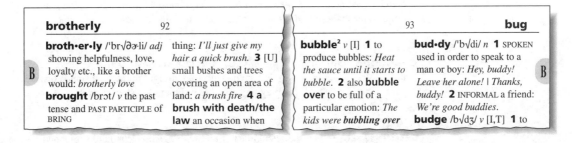

| **brotherly** | 92 | | 93 | **bug** |

broth·er·ly /ˈbrʌðəli/ *adj* showing helpfulness, love, loyalty etc., like a brother would: *brotherly love*
brought /brɔt/ *v* the past tense and PAST PARTICIPLE of BRING

thing: *I'll just give my hair a quick brush.* **3** [U] small bushes and trees covering an open area of land: *a brush fire* **4 a brush with death/the law** an occasion when

bubble² *v* [I] **1** to produce bubbles: *Heat the sauce until it starts to bubble.* **2** also **bubble over** to be full of a particular emotion: *The kids were bubbling over*

bud·dy /ˈbʌdi/ *n* **1** SPOKEN used in order to speak to a man or boy: *Hey, buddy! Leave her alone!* | *Thanks, buddy!* **2** INFORMAL a friend: *We're good buddies.*
budge /bʌdʒ/ *v* [I,T] **1** to

a. Check the words that would be found on dictionary pages with each set of guidewords:

1. **either/element**

    ____ eldest   ____ elastic   ____ elegant   ____ effect

2. **iron/isolation**

    ____ irrelevant   ____ issue   ____ isolate   ____ irony

3. **appreciation/Arabic**

    ____ apron   ____ argument   ____ appraise   ____ approve

b. Check the words that would not *be found on dictionary pages with these guidewords:*

1. **string/strong**

    ____ struck   ____ stroll   ____ strip   ____ strike

2. **yen/yours**

    ____ yield   ____ yellow   ____ youngster   ____ youth

2. Meanings

Since many words in English have more than one meaning, the dictionary lists all of them. Look at the dictionary entry for *spoil*. You will see three different meanings.

Entry
word ↓   ┌ pronunciation   part of
                            speech ↓   ┌ meanings

spoil /spɔɪl/ *v.* **spoiled** *or* **spoilt** /spɔɪlt/, **spoiled** *or* **spoilt, spoiling 1** [T] to ruin something by making it less attractive, enjoyable, useful etc.: *Don't let his bad mood spoil your evening.* **2** [I] to start to decay: *The meat has spoiled.* **3** [T] to treat someone in a way that is very kind or too generous: *a hotel that spoils its guests*

Work in small groups. Use the dictionary entry for *spoil* and the dictionary definitions for the words below to look up the meanings for the underlined word in each sentence on the next page. Write the definition that best fits the meaning of the sentence.

or•gan /ˈɔrgən/ *n* **1** part of the body of an animal or plant that has a particular purpose: *the heart, liver, and other internal organs* **2** a large musical instrument like a piano, with large pipes to make the sound, or an electric instrument that makes similar sounds

di•a•mond /ˈdaɪmənd, ˈdaɪə-/ *n* [C,U] **1** a clear, very hard, valuable stone, used in jewelry and in industry: *a diamond ring* **2** a shape with four straight points that stands on one of its points —see picture at SHAPE[1] **3** a playing card with red diamond shapes on it

set•ting /ˈsɛt̬ɪ/ *n* [C usually singular] **1** all the things that surround someone or something: *a cabin in a mountain setting* **2** a position of the controls on a machine, piece of electronic equipment etc.: *Turn the microwave to its highest setting.* **3** the place or time in which the events in a book or movie happen: *London is the setting for his most recent novel.*

poach /poʊtʃ/ *v* **1** [T] to cook food such as eggs or fish in slightly boiling liquid **2** [I,T] to illegally catch or shoot animals, birds, or fish, especially from private land

so•cial /ˈsoʊʃəl/ *adj* **1** relating to human society and its organization, or the quality of people's lives: *We ought to be dealing with the real social issues such as unemployment.* **2** relating to the position in society that you have: *friends from different social backgrounds* **3** relating to the things that you do with other people, especially for enjoyment: *Ellis always had an active social life.* **4** social animals live together in groups, rather than alone —**socially** *adv*

Appendix 8   Above material from: *Ready to Read Now*

Example
Please put the cheese back in the refrigerator before it <u>spoils</u>.

spoil = to start to decay

1. Ever since I moved to New York, my <u>social</u> life has been great.

_____

2. Can you change the <u>settings</u> on the radio in my car?

_____

3. She won the game with an ace of <u>diamonds</u>.

_____

4. He played the <u>organ</u> for our concert.

_____

5. Mrs. Lang <u>spoils</u> her children.

_____

6. The <u>setting</u> of the movie is Toronto.

_____

7. Her husband gave her beautiful <u>diamond</u> earrings for her birthday.

_____

8. The government has increased the penalty for <u>poaching</u> animals in this area.

_____

Appendix 9

106 Target Achievement Goals (TAGs)

It is essential for you to write well in English. So, we have set **T**arget **A**chievement **G**oals—**TAGs**—which are important objectives for your writing. We are focusing on the basics so that everyone will understand your writing. At ELS, you will work on your writing skills, using the TAGs to write good, clear, accurate sentences. Use these TAGs every time you write, and your writing will improve.

We want you to pay attention to these details:

- **TAG 1—The Topic:** *Your writing assignment has to address the topic*—this means that you must be sure that you write about the topic that your teacher gives you. If your writing does not address the topic, you will not meet your TAG.

- **TAG 2—Subjects and Verbs:** *All of your sentences must have subjects and verbs.* **Check your sentences for missing verbs or subjects.** *If you have 2 sentences missing verbs, or two sentences missing subjects, or one of each, you will not meet your TAG. If you have the same mistake many times, your teacher will count it as <u>a different mistake</u> each time.*

  Wrong: He a doctor. (missing verb) **Right:** He <u>is</u> a doctor.
  Wrong: Is a book on the table. (missing subject) **Right:** <u>There</u> is a book on the table.

- **TAG 3—Verb Tenses:** *All of your sentences must use the correct tenses in the correct forms.* **Check every verb in every sentence.** *If you have 2 sentences with incorrect tenses or incorrect forms, you will not meet your TAG. If you have the same mistake many times, your teacher will count it as <u>a different mistake</u> each time.* Tenses you should be able to use correctly by the end of 106: <u>simple present</u>, <u>present continuous</u>, <u>simple past</u>, <u>simple future with will</u> and <u>be going to</u>; <u>simple present perfect</u> and <u>simple past perfect</u>; and <u>passive voice, simple present uses</u>.

  Wrong: I shop for clothes yesterday. (wrong tense) **Right:** I <u>shopped</u> for clothes yesterday.
  Wrong: John going to Denver. (incomplete tense form) **Right:** John <u>is going</u> to Denver.

- **TAG 4—Word Order:** *All of your sentences must have the correct word order.* **Check every sentence for word order.** *If you have 2 sentences with mistakes in word order—statements, questions, or negatives—you will not meet your TAG. If you have the same mistake many times, your teacher will count it as <u>a different mistake</u> each time.*

Wrong: She studied her lessons last night at home hard. (statement) **Right:** She studied her lessons <u>hard at home last night</u>.
Standard Statement Word Order:
    Subject+Verb+Object+Manner Adverb+Place Adverb+Time Adverb
Wrong: Did Tom mailed the letter? (question) **Right:** Did Tom <u>mail</u> the letter?
Standard Question Word Order:
    Operator+Subject+Base Form of Verb+Object+Manner Adverb+Place
    Adverb+Time Adverb
Wrong: I no have my pencil today. (negative) **Right:** I <u>don't</u> have my pencil today.
Standard Negative Statement Word Order:
    Subject+Negative Operator+Base Form of Verb+Object+Manner Adverb+Place
    Adverb+Time Adverb

- **TAG 5—Capitalization and Punctuation:** *The first word of all of your sentences must begin with a capital letter. Proper nouns should be capitalized. Use correct punctuation at the end of your sentences.* **Check all of your sentences for capitalization and punctuation.** *If you have 3 errors in capitalization and/or punctuation you will not meet your TAG. If you have the same mistake many times, your teacher will count it as <u>a different mistake</u> each time.*

Wrong: the house is red (beginning capital; final period) **Right:** The house is red.
Wrong: robert and i fish in lake como (capitalize names of specific people and places; capitalize "I"; use final punctuation) **Right:** Robert and I fish in Lake Como.

- **TAG 6—Spelling:** *You must spell all of the words on the list of the 100 Most Common Words for Spelling correctly.* **Check your spelling; use the list.** *If you have 3 mistakes in spelling any of the 100 words, you will not meet your TAG. If you have the same mistake many times, your teacher will count it as <u>a different mistake</u> each time.*

Wrong: Meny people know wear I live. **Right:** <u>Many</u> people know <u>where</u> I live.

For Your Regular Classroom Assignments

If your paper *meets* all of your TAGs:

- Your teacher will correct it, grade it and give it back to you.
- You can rewrite it in class.
- After you rewrite your paper, you will give it back to the teacher with the original by the next class.
- You can receive up to 5 more points on your writing assignment grade for your revision.
- **You <u>must</u> revise your writing assignment. If you do not revise your paper, your grade for the entire writing assignment will be 0.**

If your paper *does not meet* one or more of your TAGs:

- **Your teacher will stop reading.**
- **Your paper will <u>fail</u>,** *but* **you will have one chance to correct it.**
- Your teacher will show you your mistakes so that **you can fix your paper.**
- You **have to** fix your paper the **same** day the teacher gives it back to you.
- **You may <u>not</u> take your paper home.**
- Fix the mistakes your teacher showed you by rewriting the problem sentences correctly. **You can completely rewrite your paper <u>only</u> if your teacher tells you that you did not address the topic.**
- Your teacher will tell you when and where you can fix your paper.

    Appendix 9   Above material from: *ELS Language Centers*

- After you fix your paper, give it back to the teacher.
- If you reach your TAGs after you fix your mistakes, the teacher will correct and grade your paper.
- The teacher will give it back to you to rewrite.
- After you rewrite your paper, you will give it back to the teacher with the original by the next class.
- **You <u>must</u> revise your writing assignment. If you do not revise your paper, your grade for the entire writing assignment will be 0. If you did not reach your TAGs the first time, you are not eligible for the additional 5 points.**
- **If you do not reach your TAGs after you fix your mistakes, your paper will fail.**

For Your Final Writing Exam

If your paper meets all of your TAGs, your teacher will

- grade your exam.
- **not correct it.**
- tell you what your final exam grade is for your writing test, but will not give you back your paper to keep.
- give you the writing rubrics form for your writing exam, which will show where your strengths and weaknesses are.
- make comments on the writing rubrics form about how you can improve your writing.
- discuss your writing exam with you during the last class of the session.

If your paper does not meet any <u>one</u> of your TAGs

- **Your teacher will stop reading.**
- Your paper will **fail**.
- There will be **no** chance to fix it.
- You will fail the exam.
- You will fail your Writing course.
- Your overall grade for your Writing course will be 0.5.
- You will repeat the level.
- Your teacher will give you the writing rubric form for your writing exam, which shows which TAGs you did not reach.
- Your teacher will discuss your paper with you during the last class of the session.

If you have any questions about this, talk to the teacher any time during the course and before the final exam; he or she will be happy to help you.

LEVEL 104 WRITING EVALUATION

Teacher: Date: Student:

☐ Addresses topic   ☐ Does not address topic

	Above standard	Standard	Below standard	Unsatisfactory	Teacher comments
Grammatical accuracy	30 **Perfect control of time and voice.** Accurate use of pronouns, articles, adjectives and all verb forms including "to be."	24 **No problems with basic forms,** including s-v-o order, present, past, future, and all forms of "to be". Well-formed compound sentences. No run on sentences.	21 Most sentences follow basic grammar rules, but **with error.** No sentence has more than one grammatical error (based on level 4 standards).	0 **Frequent grammatical errors** cause the reader to have to guess at meaning. May have impressive attempts at higher level structures, but important gaps exist in basic grammar.	
Vocabulary/ Spelling	20 Vocabulary is **varied,** ranging beyond that taught in level 4. Few errors in word choice. Correct use of some collocations and phrases. No spelling errors.	16 Uses **vocabulary specific to topic.** Uses prepositions and prepositional phrases, although with some errors. No spelling errors, except for less familiar words.	12 Essay is **simplistic** because the **vocabulary range is not sufficient.** All sentences are comprehensible. No more than one spelling error per sentence. All are phonetically recognizable.	0 **Confusing word choices** and/or excessive spelling errors make the essay difficult to understand.	
Length	10 More than 250 words, allowing for ample exploration of supporting ideas.	8 More than 150 words. Paragraphs are of a sufficient length to allow for adequate exploration of supporting ideas.	7 125 or more words, inadequate for exploration of supporting ideas.	0 Fewer than 125 words.	
3-paragraph form	10 Correct use of introduction/body/ conclusion format. Introduction leads to thesis. Body paragraph contains appropriate topic sentence. Conclusion sums up the theme. **Perfect 3-paragraph format** with appropriate linking words.	8 Has basic introduction, body and conclusion. **Correct paragraph format.**	7 Has basic introduction & body but may be missing conclusion. Essay is divided into 3 paragraphs, although with **errors in formatting.**	0 **May not use intro-body-conclusion format.** No attempt to use correct paragraph formation.	
Topic development	10 Essay has a **clear overall organization** that provides a clear exploration of the topic. Many supporting details are provided to enhance the development.	8 Topic is **adequately** explored and examples are provided. However, examples need more supporting details and specificity.	7 Topic is explored and examples are provided, but one significant area is weakened due to **lack of details.**	0 Topic is **not fully developed** or does not reach a conclusion. Thesis may not be supported in following development.	
Signal words	10 Signal words are **used correctly**— neither over nor underused. Range beyond what is taught in class.	8 Effective use of signal words as **taught** in class, although they may be overused.	6 Signal words are used, but **incorrectly.**	0 **No** use of signal words.	
Punctuation/ Capitalization	10 **Correct use** of all punctuation and capitalization rules.	8 Accurate use of **basic punctuation,** including punctuation rules and clauses as taught in class.	6 Shows an awareness of capitalization and punctuation rules as taught in class, but **with error.**	0 Capitalization and punctuation are used, but **with frequent errors.**	

Total points: _____ /100   Teacher's Initials: _____   Revision/2nd draft: _____ /100 (up to 5 points; not for final exam)

LEVEL 105 WRITING EVALUATION

Teacher: Date: Student:

☐ Addresses topic   ☐ Does not address topic

	Above standard	Standard	Below standard	Unsatisfactory	Teacher comments
Grammatical accuracy	30 **Perfect control of time and voice.** Accurate use of pronouns, articles, adjectives and all verb forms including "to be."	24 **Accurate use of all basic grammatical forms.** Uses compound sentences with some basic subordination, but clauses may not be in agreement. May have minor repeated errors based on L1 (e.g. articles).	21 **Most sentences follow basic grammar rules, but with error.** No sentence has more than one grammatical error (based on level 5 standards).	0 Many sentences have **basic grammatical errors** (S-V agreement, verb form, pronoun agreement, run on sentences, etc.) The reader must guess at meanings. May have impressive attempts at higher level structures, but important gaps exist in basic grammar.	
Vocabulary	20 Vocabulary is **varied and accurate.** Word choices throughout the essay are targeted to enhance topic development. No spelling errors.	16 Although **some errors in word choice, there is variety in vocabulary** that enhances the topic. Only occasional misspellings of phonetically irregular words.	12 Although essay is easily understandable, **limited vocabulary or spelling errors** handicap topic development. Vocabulary may be repetitive or simplistic. No more than one spelling error per sentence.	0 **Confusing word choices** AND/OR spelling errors make essay difficult to understand; OR, vocabulary is too simplistic to fully address the topic.	
Length	13 More than 275 words, **sufficient for ample exploration** of supporting ideas.	10 More than 175 words. Paragraphs are of a sufficient length to allow for **adequate exploration of supporting ideas.**	9 More than 125 words, **inadequate for exploration** of supporting ideas.	0 Fewer than 125 words.	
Introduction/ Thesis statement	13 Intro clearly leads to the thesis statement. Statement is **clear,** predictive and leads the reader into the topic. Reader can anticipate the essay.	10 Uses an introduction, but is awkwardly constructed and **lacks flow.** Thesis statement summarizes the topic as it is addressed in the essay. May have errors in construction.	8 **Attempt** at an introduction. One or two sentences can be identified as a thesis statement, but it does not satisfactorily predict the essay.	0 **No** introduction AND/OR no sentence(s) can be identified as a thesis statement. OR, statement is too general or too specific.	
4/5 paragraph development	12 Topic is **fully developed** over 4–5 paragraphs, each having a clear role. Internal organization is controlled within and between paragraphs. Each paragraph has a topic sentence that is developed with good supporting evidence.	10 Topic is developed using **standard** intro-development-conclusion, 4–5 paragraph format. Each body paragraph has a topic sentence that relates to the body of the paragraph. Some evidence and examples are supplied.	8 Topic is **not fully developed.** May have only 3 paragraphs. OR, conclusion may be too brief or inadequate. Internal development may be incomplete or missing in one key area.	0 Only **partial development** of topic. Key areas are unexplored. Fewer than 3 paragraphs. OR, does not apply paragraph formatting. OR, no conclusion.	
Signal words	12 Signal words are used correctly and **range beyond what is taught in class.** Words are chosen effectively and are used with effect.	10 Signal words are used **as taught in class** although usage may not be smooth. Punctuation is perfect.	8 Signal words are used; although some may be **used incorrectly.** OR, signal words are incorrectly punctuated.	0 No use, or mostly **incorrect use,** of signal words.	

Total points: _____ /100   Teacher's Initials: _____   Revision/2nd draft: _____   /100 (up to 5 points; not for final exam)

LEVEL 106 WRITING EVALUATION

Teacher: _____   Date: _____   Student: _____

☐ Addresses topic   ☐ Does not address topic

☐ Meets TAGs   ☐ Does not meet TAGs because of ☐ 2x missing subject/verb ☐ 2x verb tense ☐ 2x sentence pattern ☐ 3x cap/punct ☐ 3x spell-100

	Above standard	Standard	Below standard	Unsatisfactory	Teacher comments
Grammatical accuracy	30 **No errors** in all forms taught in levels 1-6.	24 **Majority of sentences have error free** use of forms taught up to level 6. Problems will still occur with phrasal verbs, and adverb clauses. May have minor repeated errors based on L1 (e.g. articles).	21 **Most sentences follow basic grammar rules, but with error.** No sentence has more than one grammatical error (based on level 6 grammar).	0 **Frequent grammatical errors** obscure meaning. May have run-on sentences. Errors in basic S-V agreement, and elementary tenses. May have impressive attempts at higher level structures, but important gaps in basic grammar.	
Vocabulary	20 Vocabulary is **varied and accurate.** Word choices are targeted to enhance topic development. Good variation of word form. No spelling errors.	16 Variety in vocabulary allows for **clear supporting details and opinions.** Evidence of some control of word form. Only minor spelling errors in phonetically irregular words.	12 Although essay is easily understandable, **vocabulary limitations** impede full topic development. May be repetitive. All sentences are comprehensible. No more than one spelling error per sentence.	0 Confusing or **simplistic** word choices limit topic development and make the essay difficult to understand. May have excessive spelling errors.	
Length/Format	10 More than 300 words. 4-5 paragraph organization, sufficient length to allow for ample exploration of supporting ideas.	8 More than 200 words. 4-5 paragraph organization. Paragraphs are sufficient length to allow for adequate exploration of supporting ideas.	7 Between 175 and 200 words. OR fewer than 4-5 paragraphs, inadequate for exploration of supporting ideas.	0 Fewer than 175 words. OR, fewer than 3 paragraphs. OR, essay lacks overall paragraphing format.	
Introduction/ Thesis statement	10 Introduction is **well crafted,** leading directly to thesis statement. Thesis is a concise, well-constructed sentence that relates to all of the main points of the essay.	8 Introduction provides background, leading to the thesis. Thesis is **clear** and presents a basis for the main points of the essay.	7 Introduction may be **awkwardly formed** and does not build to the thesis.	0 No introduction or no thesis. OR, thesis is unrelated to essay. OR, thesis is **not clear**—too general or too specific.	
4-5 paragraph development	10 Topic **fully developed** over 4-5 paragraphs, each having clear role-intro, development, and conclusion. Internal organization is controlled within and between paragraphs. Each paragraph has topic sentence and good supporting details.	8 Topic is developed using **standard** intro-development-conclusion. 4-5 paragraph format. Each body paragraph has a topic sentence that relates to the body of the paragraph. Some detail is provided.	7 Topic is **not fully developed.** May have only 3 paragraphs. OR, conclusion may be too brief or inadequate. Internal development may be incomplete or missing in one key area.	0 Only **partial development** of topic. Key areas are unexplored. Fewer than 3 paragraphs. OR, does not apply paragraph formatting. OR, no conclusion.	
Signal words	10 Signal words and related punctuation are chosen effectively and are **used flawlessly.**	8 Signal words and related punctuation are used correctly **within and between** paragraphs.	6 Signal words are used, but **limited** and without good effect. OR, repeated errors in punctuation of signal words.	0 **No** application or greatly inadequate use of signal words. OR signal words are inserted without meaning.	
Conclusion	10 Thorough, **well constructed** conclusion. Goes beyond a simple retelling of the essay. All points have been taken into consideration.	8 The conclusion provides a **basic** summary of the main points of the essay.	6 The conclusion summarizes most of the basic points of the essay. May be **overly general or too specific.**	0 Essay does **not** reach a conclusion. OR, conclusion is unrelated to the essay.	

Total points: _____ /100   Teacher's Initials: _____   Revision/2nd draft: _____ /100 (up to 5 points; not for final exam)

Above material from: *ELS Language Centers*